'The NASUWT has a long history of campaigning against homophobia and transphobia in schools and of promoting LGBT equality. All schools need effective strategies for identifying and tackling homophobia. Prejudice damages lives and adversely affects health and well-being. No child's life chances should be blighted by bullying. Schools and teachers will find *That's So Gay!* a useful resource which provides clear, practical advice and guidance on identifying the signs of homophobia. Importantly, it also raises awareness of the impact this has on those who are bullied and suggests preventive measures. It will enable schools to develop and implement effective anti-bullying policies for the whole school community.'

— *Chris Keates, NASUWT General Secretary, The Teachers' Union*

'I know I have been guilty in the past of being a teacher that has occasionally "tactically ignored" the very comment that makes up the title of this book; this fact made reading it uncomfortable at times. The stark facts around the impact of homophobic bullying paired with the practical advice have made *That's So Gay!* an agent for change in my school.'

— *Vic Goddard, Principal of Passmores Academy and star of* Educating Essex

'This book provides a wealth of useful information and guidance for schools about homophobic bullying. It is incumbent upon schools to challenge homophobia and homophobic attitudes. Bullying of LGB pupils by their peers can only be resolved through education.'

— *Christine Blower, General Secretary, National Union of Teachers*

'Charlesworth reminds us that simply saying "homophobic bullying will not be tolerated" will not magically lead to a change in attitudes. Instead he shows how to educate pupils to understand the meaning and impact of their behaviour, guiding them towards alternative behaviour and grounding them morally, ethically and socially. Gay pupils are often offered few opportunities to acquire coping strategies or learn how to be resilient in the face of homophobic bullying or name-calling. This book focuses on celebrating achievements in the school as a whole in combatting prejudice-driven bullying, and fostering a positive culture so that no pupil has to live a life out of authenticity – in which lies are told to others (and even oneself) about who one "is". This is essential reading for senior leaders, governors and staff.'

– Adrienne Katz, Director of Youthworks Consulting Ltd

THAT'S SO GAY!

of related interest

Cyberbullying and E-safety
What Educators and Other Professionals Need to Know
Adrienne Katz
ISBN 978 1 84905 276 4
eISBN 978 0 85700 575 5

Cyberbullying
Activities to Help Children and Teens to Stay Safe in a
Texting, Twittering, Social Networking World
Vanessa Rogers
ISBN 978 1 84905 105 7
eISBN 978 0 85700 228 0

E-Safety for the i-Generation
Combating the Misuse and Abuse of Technology in Schools
Nikki Giant
ISBN 978 1 84905 944 2
eISBN 978 0 85700 774 2

The KidsKope Peer Mentoring Programme
A Therapeutic Approach to Help Children and Young
People Build Resilience and Deal with Conflict
Nina Wroe and Penny McFarlane
Foreword by Andrea Ayres
ISBN 978 1 84905 500 0
eISBN 978 0 85700 903 6

Implementing Restorative Practices in Schools
A Practical Guide to Transforming School Communities
Margaret Thorsborne and Peta Blood
ISBN 978 1 84905 377 8
eISBN 978 0 85700 737 7

Surviving Girlhood
Building Positive Relationships, Attitudes and Self-
Esteem to Prevent Teenage Girl Bullying
Nikki Giant and Rachel Beddoe
ISBN 978 1 84905 925 1
eISBN 978 0 85700 704 9

Friendship and Other Weapons
Group Activities to Help Young Girls Aged 5–11 to Cope with Bullying
Signe Whitson
ISBN 978 1 84905 875 9
eISBN 978 0 85700 540 3

Life Coaching for Kids
A Practical Manual to Coach Children and Young
People to Success, Well-being and Fulfilment
Nikki Giant
ISBN 978 1 84905 982 4
eISBN 978 0 85700 884 8

"THAT'S SO GAY!

Challenging
Homophobic
Bullying

SO

GAY!

JONATHAN CHARLESWORTH

Jessica Kingsley *Publishers*
London and Philadelphia

Box 6.3 on p. 85 reproduced under the terms of the Open Government Licence v2.0.

First published in 2015
by Jessica Kingsley Publishers
73 Collier Street
London N1 9BE, UK
and
400 Market Street, Suite 400
Philadelphia, PA 19106, USA

www.jkp.com

Library of Congress Cataloging in Publication Data
Charlesworth, Jonathan, 1966-
That's so gay! : challenging homophobic bullying / Jonathan Charlesworth.
pages cm
Includes bibliographical references and index.
ISBN 978-1-84905-461-4 (alk. paper)
1. Homophobia. 2. Bullying. I. Title.
HQ76.4.C533 2015
306.76'6--dc23
2014027399

British Library Cataloguing in Publication Data
A CIP catalogue record for this book is available from the British Library

ISBN 978 1 84905 461 4
eISBN 978 0 85700 837 4

Printed and bound in Great Britain

I should like to dedicate this book to all those young people, homophobically bullied, who have not made it: those for whom their bullying was ultimately insufferable. If this book prevents one further death as a result of homophobic bullying it will have been entirely worth its writing. This book is both in memory of all those young people who have died needlessly and for you, the reader, to put to its very best use today.

Contents

Acknowledgements

First I should like to acknowledge Graham Welch, Peter Aggleton, Lynn Raphael-Reed and Debbie Epstein, whose inspiration since initial teacher training in the 1980s has led ultimately to my writing this book. Second, I would like to thank the literally thousands of colleagues (and parents) in education plus myriad other disciplines and organisations at home and abroad whose hands-on experience or strategies, both to inform the challenging of homophobic bullying and support gay young people, has informed my knowledge and expertise immeasurably over the years. You are too numerous to mention; you know who you are and I should especially like to thank the motivational Rob Wagland, Assistant Headteacher at Wyedean School, Gloucestershire and Susie Davis, Director of Student Support, Bradley Stoke Community School. Third, I would like to thank my exceptional colleagues at EACH who, with me, have made *That's So Gay! Challenging Homophobic Bullying* a reality: Vincent Puhakka, Ele Lloyd, Dave Brown, Adrian Andrews and especially my Editorial Assistant, Kate Marston. Finally, I wish to thank sincerely all my friends and loved ones for the ongoing support they have demonstrated during this book's writing.

Preface

This book is an explanation of and a practical guide to challenging homophobic language, name-calling and bullying. In its writing, it felt disingenuous to 'bolt on' transphobia and transphobic bullying to homophobia and homophobic bullying. Gender identity warrants its own focus and book. I urge more work to be done around transphobic bullying and I have colleagues who are working on upcoming resources. This will complement efforts to collectively challenge homophobic bullying and bolster our striving to create a safer and fairer society for everyone.

Aside from directly relevant references to transgender people, Appendix 2 will signal you to places where you can source help and support concerning transphobic bullying and matters regarding gender identity.

Where reference is made to 'gay people' or 'gay pupils', lesbian and bisexual adults and young people are included. Similarly homophobia includes biphobia. 'Parents' includes grandparents, carers and guardians. 'Pupils' includes learners and students. 'Governors' includes trustees. 'Sexuality' and 'sexual orientation' are used interchangeably. The named audience throughout this book is schools but if you are a college tutor, university lecturer, youth worker or someone who works in any children's service the messages are equally applicable to your own work and young people.

Introduction

There is no doubt that huge strides have been made for gay people in the UK and the USA in the last fifteen years and even since I co-authored *Safe to Learn: Homophobic Bullying* in 2007 for the Department for Children, Schools and Families (DCSF) as the Department for Education (DfE) was called at the time.

In the UK especially we have witnessed a raft of legislative progress affecting gay, transgender and heterosexual people. Starting with the equalisation of the age of consent in 1999, through enhancements to adoption and fostering rights, workplace protections, the introduction of civil partnerships in 2005 and same-sex marriage in 2014, landmark legal changes are now waiting for society to catch up with what these changes 'mean'. Not everyone, of course, is in favour of such changes. They do not see them as societal 'improvements'. Elements of the right wing press, some faith schools and even a number of our biggest institutions can at times demonstrate an alarming display of what may best be described as ignorance about what it means to be gay in 2015. Outside of the coastal cities in the USA this situation is arguably amplified.

What is ironic is that although one would think schools would be places where one would see lots of discussion and 'ground breaking' when it comes to equalities issues, they are actually very conservative places which are always *behind* change never *ahead* of it (DeWitt, 2012). This is why issues of sexuality and gender identity rarely get discussed except when raised by forward-looking teachers who usually have a personal connection with the issue which has brought it into their consciousness or there is a problem with which to be dealt.

Since 1999, UK society has witnessed landslide and welcome legislative changes advancing equalities rights and creating a more equal workplace for people who are gay. Legal improvements have increased gay people's sense of belonging to 'mainstream' society rather than feeling, as they have for too long, invisible, excluded and often ostracised from it.

We have seen this change reflected in law, the media, television, film and print advertising. One of the results of this is that gay young people are more confident about 'coming out' (acknowledge being gay, lesbian or bisexual) whilst pupils at school rather than waiting until in the workplace, college or university. We should recognise that pupils are expressing their sexual identity at a younger age than at any time in modern history (facilitated by sexting and online pornography consumption) but gay young people are accordingly coming out at a younger age – affirmed as they are by positive role models such as Tom Daley and Ellen Page and changes in legislation which they see around them.

A problem arises since although coming out is happening sooner it remains problematic for many school-age people to 'be cool' about a friend or peer being gay. I have lost count of the number of teachers who have reassured me 'but Jason has *heaps* of friends!' – who *all* turn out to be girls. What this means is that Jason does not benefit from a balance of friends (by gender). He is coping *strategically* with a problem. He is not thriving and integrated even if at the time he and his teachers fail to recognise this.

A dichotomy exists between the gay individuals and characters young people enjoy watching on television – Alan Carr, Graham Norton, Gok Wan, Little Britain, the Catherine Tate Show, Sacha Baron Cohen (as 'Bruno'), Chris Colfer (Kurt in 'Glee'), 'guests' in the *Big Brother* house – and having that reality in their classroom or actually at home in their living room or bedroom. Young people often like to give the impression they know everything they need to know and what they do not know is dull, boring or uninteresting – usually described as gay. Many young people however experience the wider world in the main through handheld devices, desktop PCs and television. Their first encounter with a gay person can in many instances be a virtual not a real one whilst their initial opportunity to make the acquaintance of a gay person 'offline' may well arrive only once they have entered the world of work or post-school study.

This dichotomy set up by media portrayals of gay identities can be particularly palpable for girls. There is an increasing concern about the impact of the media on young women and the way their lives continue to be constrained by sexual harassment: workplace discrimination, street harassment and body-shaming. All girls will be attempting to navigate the fine line set out in films, music, magazines and blogs for them to be sexy but not sexual (Tolman, 2009). This contradiction is especially evident for lesbians whose personalities are either conflated with pornography or dismissed as frigid. For a girl to come out as a lesbian or bisexual is in many ways to commit a 'double violation' as she is expressing sexual attraction and it is for the same sex (Tolman, 2009, p.185). Female pupils who come out as lesbian or bisexual are often faced with incredulity or a heightened level of sexual interest or harassment.

The registered charity, EACH (Educational Action Challenging Homophobia) supported a boy who chose to come out aged 13 and it is not at all uncommon today for young people to come out at 14 or 15 years of age. This does not mean that individuals are not fearful of the ramifications. Harassment and homophobic bullying remain a distinct possibility for too many gay young people. The younger one's peers are when someone comes out, the less is their emotional maturity to accept the revelation and adapt to the perceived drastic 'difference' in the friend 'they thought they knew'. Added to this is the potential for ostracism from parents and other loved ones. Rejection is bad enough but that by one's own parents is the most painful of all.

Each pupil attending school has the right to an education which fires the imagination and promotes the realisation of every aspect of potential available to that young person during their time there. Teachers are essentially very effective gatekeepers to this education, exerting huge power to either facilitate or block it. It is however their legal and moral duty to promote it to the best of their abilities (DeWitt, 2012).

Gay pupils deserve to be treated with the same respect as their heterosexual peers whilst at school and in anticipation of their role within adult society. Teachers have a duty of care to nurture and develop values such as empathy, understanding and respect for every pupil and towards every pupil. Teachers can help change the culture in their own classroom whilst headteachers can bring about whole school change by 'leading from the front' with confidence and conviction. Straightforward practice such as the use of appropriate language, what is placed on noticeboards (or not), on websites (or not) or the choice of outside speakers sends out powerful messages about what is valued, endorsed or matters.

Too often in schools we talk about 'LGBT issues' in terms of homophobic bullying and not in terms of 'normalising' the topic by, instead, discussing rights, respect, equality and justice. In the UK this is without doubt one of the legacies of Section 28 of the Local Government Act 1988: effectively choking off constructive discussion between teachers and pupils, pupils and pupils and teachers and teachers for years, 15 to be exact (see Appendix 1). But the cast of Section 28's shadow did not stop in 2003 in the year of its repeal. My teaching, training and consultancy to and for schools since 1985 has reflected time after time how unconfident teachers are, on a number of levels, to address matters of sexual orientation. It has come down to a brave sole teacher to pick up the issue either because they have someone in their personal life who is gay or they are attempting to support a gay pupil and so often need to reach out for support beyond the school gates and seek support from EACH or another service provider.

Bullying will continue until adults cease to model it to children so very effectively and so regularly: during Prime Minister's Questions in the House of Commons, on television programmes like BBC's *Question Time*, in reality TV shows and within sports fixtures. Children simply copy what they see adults doing – this is part of what 'growing up' means to them. The wellbeing of pupils in our schools is paramount and part of teachers' responsibilities. Schools who fail to adequately safeguard this (including from bullying and harassment) are failing to meet their responsibilities both in law and their duty of care.

Homophobic bullying is never just 'banter', a 'joke' or 'a bit of a drama'. It can cause major fear, trauma, increase the likelihood of various forms of self-harm and seriously limit aspirations and achievement. The effects of exposure to bullying can lead well into adulthood, ruining individuals' lives.

We all have the power however to do something to challenge bullying – including homophobic bullying – and I trust you will find this book a practical one to help you and your school, college or other youth setting to better understand what is homophobic or anti-gay bullying, who experiences it (and why), its impact and what you should and can do about it (and why). It will also guide you towards creating an inclusive school which prevents all forms of bullying and challenges name-calling. When children are being bullied the achievement of all or any of the Government's desired outcomes incidentally will be seriously undermined.

Along the way you will learn how to work with those who bully homophobically. Since 2000 when I started working full-time to challenge homophobic bullying and harassment, 'gay' has been the word which remains for far too many children and young adults the one of choice to put down, insult, 'diss' or cuss someone when actually it is an adjective to describe a sexual orientation or a word found in poetry, prose and music to describe brightness, jollity and cheerfulness. Our failure as adults to challenge 'gay' when used offensively (either deliberately or inadvertently) readily paves the way for homophobic bullying. So let us begin by acknowledging in every classroom that in society some people *are* gay. And let's *talk* about it.

CHAPTER 1

What is Homophobic Bullying?

Bullying is behaviour by an individual or a group usually repeated over time. Its purpose is to intentionally hurt either another individual or group emotionally and sometimes physically.

Homophobic bullying happens in both primary and secondary schools and in a variety of ways. It is a specific form of bullying occurring when bullying is motivated by prejudice against gay people, those perceived to be gay, someone with a gay relative or simply because the target is different in some way. When targeted at those identified by the perpetrator as 'different' this can be because the target does not conform to 'expected' or 'gender appropriate' behaviour. It is the person's identity which is used to abuse them and homophobic bullying can therefore be experienced by a young person regardless of their sexuality.

At its most benign it is voiced as a passive dislike of gay people. At its most destructive it involves active victimisation. Homophobic bullying is not characterised by specific acts but by the negative attitudes and beliefs towards gay people that underlie these acts. If homophobic bullying, or any form of prejudice-based bullying, is addressed solely as an issue of discipline the underlying causes will remain unchallenged.

Like all bullying, homophobic bullying can present itself in different forms: both direct and indirect. Table 1.1 comprehensively details the different ways in which bullying can be experienced

(London Borough of Wandsworth Safeguarding Children Board 2012). Direct forms of bullying include name-calling, offensive texts or tweets, comparing pupils to stereotyped gay or lesbian caricatures and, too often, violent physical assaults. Indirect forms of bullying may include rumour-mongering, being left out or vandalism. This abuse can take place in school halls, classrooms, playgrounds, at youth centres or after school clubs and even in the privacy of one's bedroom via the internet or mobile phones.

Homophobic language is frequently used without its perpetrators thinking and is often ignored because it can be difficult to know how to respond without awareness and appropriate training. Homophobic language is regularly brushed off as 'harmless banter' and not thought to be particularly hurtful. Homophobic language and attitudes in schools need to be challenged however because ignoring them allows homophobic bullying to gain a foothold, continue, then escalate.

Homophobic language and abuse starts in primary school where pupils may call each other, or indeed inanimate objects, 'gay' without really understanding what this means. If such use is not challenged at this stage it will appear acceptable making it more difficult to address in secondary school. Children may also experience verbal bullying because they have a gay parent or sibling. It is very common for a primary school to first 'meet' homophobic bullying when one of its pupils is found to have 'two mums'.

Pupils can also experience indirect homophobic abuse, not directed towards a particular person or group, but when remarks are made to pass negative judgement such as 'rounders is gay' or 'your ringtone is so gay'. It is important for all staff to challenge pupils and explain the consequences of using 'gay' in a derogatory way. It might be time consuming at first but a consistent approach in challenging such language is vital to achieving progress and the creation of an environment in which being gay is not thought of in negative terms.

Direct homophobic abuse is directed towards an individual or group of pupils as a one-off incident or repeatedly. A boy who is called 'poof' or hears 'faggot' when he walks by, or a girl who is called a 'dyke' or a 'lezzer' and avoided as she walks through the school corridor can suffer both short- and long-term harm.

In secondary school, homophobic language might be extensive and used directly or indirectly to:

- ridicule or denigrate something considered inferior or risible – 'Circle Time's so gay!'

- harass a pupil with a gay parent, sibling or in-law – 'Your dad left you 'cos he's a gay boy!'

- use sexuality as a way to disparage the actions of another – 'You like One Direction? They are well gay!'

- imply a response to a call to action is unacceptable – 'It's a show I'd have to sing in? That's too gay, man!'

- intimidate someone or make them feel uncomfortable – 'Sir, do you like musicals?'

- undermine and bully someone by suggesting that they are gay, including spreading rumours and malicious gossip – 'Samira's so hairy! She gotta be a lesbian!'

- verbally bully someone who is gay, or who is thought to be gay – 'Got your little clarinet, have you? You are flippin' gay!'

Homophobic bullying increasingly takes place through cyberbullying, i.e. phone calls, text messaging, picture/video messaging, email, online message boards, online chat rooms and in personal web spaces. Through modern technology, vicious comments can be made and rumours spread about a person's sexual orientation. Whole communities become bystanders as these incidents largely go unreported. Advances in technology have transformed the bullying landscape with new tools such as Smartphones and screen-grabbing mobile phone applications ('apps') providing platforms to target pupils directly or indirectly 24 hours a day, seven days a week. This can make it harder for educators and parents to recognise when it is going on. Schools need to ensure that they are alert to the risks of cyberbullying and include provision for it within their anti-bullying policies.

TABLE 1.1 THE WAYS IN WHICH BULLYING CAN BE EXPERIENCED

Behaviour	Personal aspects	Social aspects	Criminal
Verbal bullying that is deliberately intended to hurt, intimidate, frighten, harm or exclude	• name-calling, belittling comments, jokes or verbal attacks based on appearance, home situation, sexuality, family • nasty teasing • hurting a person's feelings • sexual harassment • making personal threats	• alienating a person from their friends and social groups • damaging a reputation • excluding and not including in small or larger group activities • spreading rumours • using sexually abusive or suggestive language to exclude a person or group • ostracising • malicious gossiping	• coercing people or daring them to do illegal acts • inciting others to do dangerous things • inciting hatred towards an individual or group • homophobic, transphobic or sexist/sexual harassment • threats about damaging a person, their family, friends or property, including inflicting physical harm • intimidating telephone calls • homophobic taunting • sexist taunting
Non-verbal bullying that is deliberately intended to hurt, intimidate, harm, exclude or frighten	• intimidation through gesture • hiding, stealing or damaging a person's books or belongings • dirty looks • sending written threats	• setting someone up to take the blame publicly • shunning someone – not speaking with or interacting with them • 'kissing teeth' (to express disapproval by clicking one's tongue behind one's teeth)	• theft • stalking

Physical bullying includes: • a direct physical attack on a person • an indirect attack on property or belongings	• beating • biting • choking • kicking • punching • shaking • slapping • tripping • spitting • hitting • poking • throwing • shoving • urinating • groping or unwanted touching • ignoring	• embarrassment and public humiliation • group bullying – when a child or young person is outnumbered or picked on in some of the following ways: - blocking the way - demanding money - being forced to participate in embarrassing initiation rites - being forced to do unwanted things in front of others - having belongings destroyed, stolen and/or ridiculed	• extortion with threats • sexual abuse • sexual violence • threatening with a weapon • using a weapon to inflict harm • physical assault • stealing • 'happy slapping' • criminal damage
Technological Bullying: the majority of verbal and non-verbal behaviours can be carried out using new forms of technology – therefore technological bullying takes the same form as non-physical victimisation, but without the bully having to confront the victim face-to-face; it is often carried out anonymously	• sending threatening or intimidating comments via email, text messages, internet forums • making malicious or prank phone calls • instant messaging • internet chat rooms • personal websites • creating web pages which aim to intimidate psychologically and/or physically threaten, or socially damage an individual or group	• taking embarrassing or humiliating pictures or video clips on mobile phones which may also be sent or shared with others • setting up or contributing to online forums or websites, where users post malicious comments about a person or group (e.g. trolling)	• using any of these technological methods to threaten, intimidate or harass an individual or group

Verbal abuse

Broadly speaking, the use of homophobic language and verbal abuse is the most common form of homophobic harassment in schools. This includes name-calling, teasing and threatening another person because of their sexuality, perceived sexuality or association with people who are lesbian, gay or bisexual.

It is regularly cited that the use of phrases such as 'That's so gay' to deem something as rubbish or inferior is 'endemic' within UK and US schools. Additionally, in the US and increasingly the UK, the phrase 'no homo' is used to distance oneself from something that inadvertently 'sounds gay' and asserts that the speaker does not have gay 'inclinations'. For example, a boy might say 'I love the new Rihanna album. No homo!' It is important to remember that homophobic verbal abuse goes beyond this cliché. One activity EACH delivers during workshops with pupils explores common insults heard throughout a typical school day and identifies which aspect of a person's identity these insults are targeting (see Box 1.1). Invariably pupils cite the regular use of language targeting someone's sexuality, weight, attractiveness, disability, race or sex.

When identifying these insults the sheer number of derogatory labels that pupils associate with being gay never ceases to surprise. In contrast, if one tasks someone with thinking of a synonym for the label heterosexual they will invariably only be able to come up with one: 'straight'. Homophobic language often includes derogatory words such as 'dyke', 'faggot' or 'queer' as well as phrases which reduce gay identities to sexual acts described in explicit or aggressive language. Of course, this language use varies depending on the setting and many pupils will be aware that it is unacceptable. As a result they may be careful not to use it in the presence of teachers or other authority figures.

> 'The trouble is people know to not say anything homophobic in front of teachers but then some say it all the time when they're out of earshot.' Sascha, 14

When one engages pupils in an honest discussion about the abuse they hear it is clear this language sits within their everyday lexicon and needs to be challenged.

Box 1.1 Activity idea: targeting differences

Divide your pupils into small groups and provide them with sticky notes. Give each group two minutes to list all the taunts and insults they regularly hear around school.

Once the pupils have listed these invite them to be grouped into aspects of 'difference'. This may include appearance, size, intelligence, skin colour, faith, sexuality, gender or physical impairment.

Once the pupils have identified these common groups ask the whole class to discuss:

- What aspect of 'difference' attracts the most insults?

- In what situations are these insults used?

- What do these insults say about what is 'normal' and 'acceptable'?

- Where might messages of what is 'normal' and 'acceptable' come from?

Establish with pupils opportunities to challenge this use of language as an individual, as a class and as a school.

Adapted from EACH (2014)

Whilst the use of 'gay' and 'That's so gay' to describe something as stupid, uncool or boring is not as overtly abusive as some of the language cited above it is no less problematic. It can be harder to challenge as it does not always accompany bullying. More often than not it is used in reference to situations or to describe objects rather than target an individual. As a result pupils may not recognise that this language use is inappropriate and argue that calling their homework gay has nothing to do with their opinions on same-sex relationships. In fact pupils who identify as gay do use this language. What these pupils should recognise is that its use reinforces implicit prejudices and derogatory labels about lesbian, gay and bisexual people (broken, worthless, wrong) against which the gay rights movement has been campaigning for very many decades (see Box 1.2). Educators should recognise that phrases such as 'That's so gay' do not exist in isolation from homophobic abuse that is played out in wider society and a simple phrase unchallenged will escalate into more overt abuse.

> **Box 1.2** Good As You
>
> The term 'gay' is used to describe both same-sex attracted men and just as often, today, women. There is wide agreement its use in this context emerged as part of the civil rights struggle of the 1960s and 1970s where, as an acronym, it spelt out 'Good As You' on marchers' banners. The banner at the time would have read 'Rights for homosexuals [sic]. We're as Good As You!'

Physical abuse

As the name suggests, physical bullying includes hitting, punching and kicking. This is arguably the most visible form of homophobic bullying and more commonly reported amongst boys who are often cited both as its targets and perpetrators. Despite this we should be wary not to dismiss this behaviour as 'boys being boys' nor regard it as exceptional when girls engage in physical bullying or boys in ostracism.

When physical bullying does occur it can be a matter for the police. This is covered in Chapter 7. Physical abuse can include inappropriate touching or sexual assault. This is less likely to be recognised or reported. Just as homophobic language can often reduce gay people to sex acts, inappropriate touching may include 'simulating' sex acts associated with being lesbian or gay. It can also include pressuring a young person to 'prove' they are not gay by kissing a girl or boy, allowing themselves to be touched or touching someone else sexually.

Relational bullying

Relational bullying refers to rumour-mongering, ignoring or ostracising with the intention of damaging friendships or relationships. This form of bullying is less visible than explicit forms such as verbal and physical abuse but no less distressing.

When pupils are ostracised four fundamental needs, according to Maslow's hierarchy of needs, are threatened:

- belonging

- self-esteem

- control

- meaningful existence.

This kind of bullying can be taking place face-to-face but it frequently manifests itself online. Pupils 'un-friending' someone on Facebook or spreading rumours via texts and social media are examples. Educators may not always recognise the very tangible impact that being ostracised online can have on a young person's relationships and friendships. All it takes is a click of a button for a rumour to 'go viral' reaching hundreds or even thousands. The impact of this on a young person's emotional wellbeing should never be underestimated.

Indirect bullying

Indirect forms of bullying may involve stealing, damage to property, graffiti or intimidating looks. On a recent visit to a school the pupils with whom EACH was working spoke of the homophobic graffiti they see on their walk to school. One example was even cited right outside the school gates.

> 'On Saturday, I walked round the neighbourhood with my granddad. We were looking for all the times we could spot homophobic graffiti. We found loads!' Brandon, 14

Cyberbullying

Cyberbullying refers to the harassment of others through digital technologies such as mobile phones, computers, tablets or other devices with the intention of causing harm either directly or indirectly. This can include abusive messages via text or social media, web pages and groups set up specifically to spread hateful messages or rumours, silent and malicious calls, blackmailing and taking photos or videos and sharing these over the internet or mobile networks without consent. The casual use of homophobic language online has also been highlighted by researchers in the USA (see Box 1.3).

Cyberbullying can have the following distinct features which set it apart from other forms of bullying:

- Impact: the scale and scope of cyberbullying can be greater than for other forms of bullying.

- Targets and perpetrators: the people involved may have a different profile to traditional bullies and their targets.

- Location: the 24/7 and 'anyplace' nature of cyberbullying is distinctive.

- Anonymity: the person being bullied will not always know who is attacking them.

- Motivation: some pupils may not be aware that what they are doing is bullying.

- Evidence: unlike other forms of bullying the target of such bullying always has the evidence.

Box 1.3 Nohomophobes.com

Nohomophobes (Wells, 2014) is a website designed by the University of Alberta's Institute for Sexual Minority Studies and Services. It was established on 5 July 2012 to be a 'social mirror' reflecting the pervasiveness of casual homophobic language in society. The website achieves this by keeping an ongoing counter of how frequently the words 'faggot', 'dyke', 'no homo' and 'so gay' are used on Twitter. As of 25 November 2014 the counter had recorded in total:

- 30,058,026 uses of faggot

- 3,592,540 uses of dyke

- 8,381,335 uses of no homo

- 8,518,190 uses of so gay.

Why is homophobic bullying the least reported form of bullying?

One of the key challenges EACH or other service providers face is that they know it goes on but homophobic bullying rarely is reported. There are a number of reasons pupils cite as to why they do not report anti-gay bullying in school.

It is often felt that to report homophobic bullying is to cast aspersions on one's sexuality. As a result pupils who may be gay but not ready to come out will be reluctant to report for fear of attracting further questioning. Similarly pupils who are heterosexual can feel that reporting homophobic bullying is akin to coming out.

A lot of pupils may be reluctant to admit that they are upset by the homophobic abuse. The desire not to be seen as weak or a victim can make pupils reluctant to report any form of bullying. For homophobic bullying this can be more palpable as it is so often dismissed as 'banter', 'a drama' or 'just a joke'. Therefore to report it would be seen to be taking it too seriously and attract further abuse.

Finally, we know that pupils are unconfident in the mechanisms schools put in place to respond to bullying. Too many feel that their teachers will not take the problem seriously. They can also be unsure how to report if homophobic bullying is not specifically cited as unacceptable within school policies and practice. In addition, pupils often cite a lack of clear and consistent sanctions in school when responding to bullying. Many fear that by reporting bullying they themselves will be excluded from activities in order to avoid being targeted by their perpetrator(s). EACH regularly hears stories of targeted pupils being asked to change separately for sports lessons, physical education or leave lessons early in order to avoid running into their tormentors. Without doubt the USA's Gay, Lesbian and Straight Education Network (GLSEN) hears similar stories.

In Chapter 2 I identify common scenarios in which pupils experience homophobic bullying. This will build upon the understanding of what homophobic bullying looks like and provide further insights as to why pupils may be reticent to report. The next chapter also highlights how anyone can become a target, regardless of sexual orientation.

Key points

- Homophobic bullying is not characterised by specific acts but by the negative attitudes and beliefs towards gay people that underlie it.

- Relational and cyberbullying can be less recognisable than verbal and physical bullying but equally damaging.

- Pupils are often unconfident that school mechanisms will effectively deal with bullying and fear reporting homophobic bullying is akin to coming out.

- Casual homophobic language is pervasive offline and online and simple phrases such as 'That's so gay' left unchallenged can escalate into more overt abuse.

- Teachers need to actively engage pupils in discussions about homophobic bullying to gain an accurate insight into pupils' attitudes and experiences of this prejudice-based bullying.

CHAPTER 2

Who Experiences Homophobic Bullying?

It can often be assumed that homophobic bullying only impacts upon lesbian, gay or bisexual pupils. The reality is that homophobia affects all young people regardless of their sexual orientation. Many pupils will experience homophobic bullying before they, or those perpetrating it, are even aware of their own sexual orientation. It is important therefore that we do not make assumptions about those involved.

Young people can hear of issues regarding sexuality from a number of sources. What they hear is often based on myth, misinformation or outright prejudice. By the time many young people come to realise whether they are attracted to the same, opposite or both sexes the very labels lesbian, gay or bisexual have been stigmatised. Therefore with the world constantly promoting heterosexuality as the norm, realising you are gay (or the assumption having been made that you are) can be a distressing experience. Stereotypes can cause young people to feel obliged to consciously or unconsciously prove that they are not gay. This curtails the freedom of expression and individuality of all young people not just those who are gay (LGBT Youth Scotland, 2006).

Ultimately every young person will experience the limiting effects of homophobic bullying be they the perpetrator, target or bystander. Challenging it is for the benefit of everyone in your school or youth setting. The values and attitudes that homophobia reinforces make it difficult for young people to appreciate the diverse people who will soon become their college or university peers, work colleagues, family members and so on. If the role of school is to prepare young people for wider society it is failure on the part of us as educators to let these values and attitudes go unchallenged.

Whilst the reasons young people experience homophobic bullying vary depending upon their specific circumstances, common motives can nevertheless be identified. Understanding why some young people are targeted over others can help schools identify the underlying beliefs that fuel this prejudice and consider ways to challenge the attitudes of perpetrators. The sections below explore case studies in order to understand the different reasons young people experience homophobic bullying.

Lesbian, gay or bisexual pupils

> 'I'm 13 and I've recently come out to my elder brother Robert. He responded really well and has been very accepting and supportive. I told Robert that I'm worried that I'll be bullied if others find out that I'm gay. I've heard of people being bullied in our school because they were gay. Some even had to move school because it got so bad. Robert told me to talk to my tutor but she just seemed really uncomfortable and sent me to the school counsellor.' Lucas, 13

Young people who are lesbian, gay or bisexual are the most vulnerable to homophobic bullying. Even if they are not the direct targets, witnessing homophobic bullying can cause negative messages and stereotypes about one's identity to become internalised. All too often young people like Lucas only ever hear about gay young people being bullied, assaulted or abused because of their sexuality. Bullying and tragedy can be seen as inevitable for gay young people. It is the responsibility of school staff to ensure all pupils feel safe and understand that homophobic bullying will not be tolerated. It is possible for gay young people to be resilient to and resist negative messages about their identity and in order to do this they require affirmative and accurate information about their lives. In Lucas's case his personal tutor did nothing to assuage his fears that he may become the target of bullying. In addition, by referring Lucas to the school counsellor his tutor implied that simply because someone is gay they need help or 'therapy'.

> 'I'm 16 and I've known I am a lesbian for over a year now. Although I have a lot of really close friends I haven't told any of them. Most of my friends are girls and absolutely boy obsessed. I feel a lot of pressure to date boys and do things that I don't want to do. I've tried to avoid it but when I do my friends say I'm frigid and stop inviting me to parties. I'm so scared that they will find out and I will lose all my friends.' Lucy, 16

Gay young people can also be vulnerable because the bullying they experience goes undetected. In Lucy's case she was ostracised for not dating boys. As a result she feels she has to hide who she is so her friends will accept her. In homophobic environments many gay young people will deny their sexual orientation to themselves or others. All too often experiences such as Lucy's can be ignored. Research suggests that being left out has stronger links to poor emotional wellbeing than more explicit forms of bullying (Benton, 2011). It is important you are aware that you may not always know who in your school is gay and we should not make assumptions about the sexual orientation of the people with whom we work. Gay people of all ages can find themselves emotionally exhausted by having to reconcile how they are feeling inside with the problems others have in understanding, recognising and coming to terms with their sexuality.

> 'When I was 15 I came out as bisexual. I only told a close set of friends but some of them told others. Rumours started to spread that I was a slut and only pretending to be bisexual to impress boys. Sometimes when classmates joke about it I get really angry and get into fights but that only ever seems to get me in trouble.' Rachel, 16

Different stigmas are attached to the labels lesbian, gay and bisexual. Young people, and adults alike, who are bisexual can face discrimination from their heterosexual, lesbian and gay peers. Rachel's experience of being called a 'slut' and the claim she is only 'pretending' is not an uncommon experience for bisexual young people. Many people see bisexuality as synonymous with promiscuity although this is not the case. The assumption that bisexual people are promiscuous can make them the target of sexual harassment and bullying. Whilst some young people who identify as bisexual will go on to identify as exclusively heterosexual, lesbian or gay many will not. All young people should have a right to come to this understanding of their sexual orientation free from abuse and harassment. It is common for the experiences of bisexual young people to be dismissed as 'just a phase'. As a result, their experience of bullying may be belittled or underestimated.

Lesbian, gay or bisexual by association

'When my partner David and I moved to a new town for my job our son had to move primary school. Since then he has been the target of homophobic bullying from the majority of his peers. The other boys call him "gay boy", exclude him from their games and tell him he has to hang out with the girls. We have reported it to the school however most of the bullying takes place on the playground so they barely notice it. He is only 11 but he has started to walk home from school by himself because he hates it when we come to pick him up. I'm concerned that the harassment will continue into secondary school.' Jimmy, parent

Pupils may become the target of homophobic bullying if they are associated with people who are gay. If they have same-sex parents, a sibling or close friend who is gay, these young people can face the same stigma attached to being gay. Once again this may cause negative messages and stereotypes about their family or friends to become internalised. This makes it difficult to associate with people who are gay due to 'guilt by association'. In Jimmy's case this is demonstrated by his son's unwillingness to be picked up from school.

Young people experiencing bullying because of their association with people who are gay are also less likely to report it. This can be because they are scared that if they report it they too will be labelled gay. It can also be however that they do not want to upset the friend or family member who is gay. Parents who have a child who is being bullied will always find this a distressing experience. For same-sex parents this can place an additional strain as homophobic bullying has historically been used to undermine the validity of lesbian and gay parenting.

It is not at all uncommon for homophobic bullying to start in primary school. Children and young people's ideas about what is and is not acceptable with regard to gender and sexual orientation form from a very early age. Whilst most children in primary school will not fully understand what homophobic language means its use communicates strong messages about what is acceptable behaviour. Too few primary schools have received training or support to address homophobic bullying robustly and may not always be aware of the role it is playing in children's bullying. Ofsted's guidance on preventing homophobic bullying requires primary schools to challenge pupils who use 'gay' pejoratively and explain why it is wrong, address bullying where pupils are picked on for not behaving like a 'typical girl' or 'typical boy' and ensure that pupils are taught about different families (Ofsted, 2014a).

Suspected of being lesbian, gay or bisexual

> 'I'm 16 years old and mostly hang out with girls rather than boys. I feel safer when I'm with a female crowd and less pressure to play sport and be aggressive. The bullying started when I was 13 as everyone said I had a 'gay voice'. Last year a classmate accused me of being gay. Now everyone has got it into their heads that I am.' Ryan, 16

Pupils can be 'suspected' of being gay for a number of reasons. Often this has a lot to do however with expectations around gender and gender roles. In Lucy's case she felt a lot of pressure to date boys and be sexually available whereas for boys the pressure can be to behave in an aggressive, 'macho' manner and position themselves in opposition to girls or gay men. Therefore in Ryan's case the strong association with girls and his disinterest in sport and aggression cast 'suspicion' on his sexuality.

Being bullied because people assume you are gay is just as damaging to young people as being bullied because you are gay. Young people may be less likely to report this type of bullying for fear of confirming the bullies' accusations. Sometimes when young people are courageous enough to report it they are met with the response: 'If you're not gay, what is the problem?' As a result the homophobic element of the bullying may not be dealt with effectively or at all.

Homophobic bullying by proxy

> 'I'm 15 years old and Sikh. I've never experienced any abuse because of my background before but recently I have been having problems. I do not shave because of my religion and every time I get ready for PE class this girl clique call me a 'hairy dyke'. My friends have offered to shave my legs for me but I don't want to give in to the pressure of a small group of girls.' Aagya, 15

Young people will experience homophobic bullying differently depending on a range of factors including gender, sexual orientation, class, faith, ethnicity and disability. For example in Aagya's case she feels the homophobic language is being used to stigmatise her expression of faith and ethnicity. Educators should be aware that homophobic language can be used as a proxy for gendered, disablist or racist prejudice. A survey of 5032 young people's experiences online found that young carers and those with special educational needs experienced far higher rates of homophobic abuse online than their peers (Katz, 2013). This can often be because homophobic language is more common, less likely to be challenged and easier to 'get away with' than other forms of prejudice-driven language.

Whilst the targeting of her faith and ethnicity appears to be Aagya's primary concern we should not assume that the homophobic element does not bother her. It is all too common for us not to consider the multiple identities of young people and particularly to presume heterosexuality amongst black and minority ethnic (BME) and disabled young people. People who experience discrimination and abuse because of their faith, ethnicity or disability may be reluctant to disclose their sexual orientation as it becomes an additional issue with which to deal. Either way it is important in cases such as Aagya's that both prejudiced attitudes are addressed and the young people involved understand that prejudice-based bullying of any kind will not be tolerated.

A lot of gay young people tell a teacher, youth worker or other adult in a position of trust before they tell a parent that they are, or think they are, gay which calls upon that adult's full duty of care, sense of responsibility and diplomacy skills if and when it comes to negotiating communications or liaisons between home and this young person.

It is vital to hold on to the fact that coming out as gay or lesbian at school can mean having precious few people to whom to turn for genuine, committed support. Pupils who can confide in understanding, caring friends are the young people you may not get to hear about except when the subject is discussed casually in your presence. Many pupils experience bullying in school so when bullying accompanies coming out it is a double edged sword: a young person needs support when coming out but often is reluctant to report anti-gay bullying. This is explored in Chapter 8.

It is not only pupils targeted by homophobic bullying who may be struggling with coming out or their perceived sexual orientation. In Chapter 3 I highlight the characteristics of pupils who engage in homophobic bullying and the transience of labels such as 'bully' and 'victim', noting that young people can be both the 'bully' and the 'victim' throughout their school experience.

Key points

- Homophobic name-calling can start as early as primary school.

- Homophobic bullying does not solely affect lesbian, gay or bisexual pupils.

- Junior or elementary schools invariably meet the issue of homophobic bullying when one of their pupils (aged around ten) experiences homophobic bullying because they have 'two mums'. Homophobia does not begin and end in our secondary schools.

- Pupils who are not gay can find homophobic bullying equally damaging.

- Young people will experience homophobic bullying differently depending on a range of factors including gender, sexual orientation, class, faith, ethnicity and disability.

CHAPTER 3

Who Perpetrates Homophobic Bullying?

Just as there is no one 'type' of person who experiences homophobic bullying there is no single 'type' of its perpetrator. Pupils from all kinds of backgrounds can engage in this prejudice-driven behaviour. They may attempt justification of their actions for a number of reasons and these are explored in more detail in Chapter 4. Explored in this chapter are common factors which have been assigned to perpetrators of homophobic bullying. These are identified not to create a discrete and distinct profile of a 'bully' but to gain a better understanding of what may cause someone to behave in this way.

Whilst we may discuss bullying in terms that categorise pupils into different roles – the perpetrator, the target or the bystander – it is important to recognise that these roles are not fixed. Pupils who have been bullied may engage in bullying themselves as a form of retaliation. Similarly a pupil can be a bystander in one incident but a perpetrator or target in another. In addition, pupils who engage in face-to-face bullying can differ greatly from those who perpetrate abuse online. As a result the distinction between a bully, a target and a bystander is rarely clear cut.

Research into bullying has indicated that both those who perpetrate and those who experience bullying share a number of common difficulties which can explain why they are involved in the experience. These include 'internalised distress' such as anxiety, depression, low self-esteem, academic problems and difficulty

41

making friends, and 'externalised distress' such as anger, oppositional behaviour and impulse control (Nansel *et al.*, 2001). Both those who bully and those who are targeted can have difficulties responding to stress and coping with conflict in peer relationships. Whilst young people who bully do report the internalising of problems it is much more common for them to exhibit externalising behaviour. In other words, in response to stress some young people may act out whilst others withdraw.

Ultimately there is no steadfast rule as to why a pupil may bully someone. Looking specifically at homophobic bullying we can identify some potential stress factors which contribute to a target's experience of this type of bullying. Once again, factors can overlap with those experiencing homophobic bullying actually doing so because of another aspect of their identity: religion, disability or culture, for example.

Sexual orientation

We rarely question the sexual orientation of those who perpetrate homophobic bullying. Much as it is often presumed that someone experiencing homophobic bullying is gay we can wrongly assume perpetrators are always heterosexual. Many young people who engage in this type of bullying behaviour will be doing so before they are confident of their own sexual orientation. Whether they are gay or heterosexual, homophobia is tied up with its perpetrator's understanding and expression of their own sexual orientation. Young people who distance themselves from gay people through homophobia can be just as much trying to affirm their identity as the girl or the boy society expects them to be, as to 'prove' their sexual orientation.

Young people grow up familiar with the stigmas attached to being gay. The negativity surrounding gay identities can lead to a conscious or unconscious desire to be seen as heterosexual whether they have a genuine comprehension of their sexual orientation or not. The expression of heterosexuality in young people often involves distancing themselves from and denigrating anything or anyone perceived to be gay. It is not simply enough to know you are attracted to the opposite sex; you have to 'prove it' through expected behaviours and rituals which can include homophobic bullying and certainly homophobic language.

This form of homophobic bullying is an expression of insecurity amongst heterosexual and gay young people alike. For young people who identify as heterosexual it can be the fear that they will lose the social advantage that this identity and its associated 'lifestyle' affords them. Heterosexuality continues to occupy dominant status anywhere in the world. For young people who identify as gay however it can be a form of 'internalised homophobia' the negative messages about being gay and its 'associated lifestyle' affect the way they view themselves and others (Aiden, Marston and Perry, 2013). This can result in the denial of their sexual orientation, feelings of inadequacy, low self-esteem or contempt for those who are gay or are perceived to be gay.

When one's standing in the world and the opportunities available are dictated by whether we love people of the same sex the insecurity this creates is oppressive. The stigma attached to being gay does not just affect those who are gay but fosters insecurity amongst heterosexual young people too, obliged as they are to present themselves in ways 'appropriate' to their gender (and being 'appropriately gendered' means one is heterosexual).

When heterosexual and gay identities are truly valued as equal we find that homophobic attitudes and behaviours fall away. No longer is one required to push others down in order to pull oneself up. We are all valued and we are all equal.

Gender

Sexual orientation is not the only factor which can place pressure on young people to behave in certain ways. Just as sexual orientation prescribes our position in society similarly so does our sex: male or female. Equally importantly, we are expected to adopt the gender roles (masculine or feminine) deemed socially acceptable to being male or female (see Box 3.1). Boys are often found to be aggressors experiencing and perpetrating physical bullying, verbal abuse and vandalism whereas girls are associated with relational bullying such as excluding others, 'bitchiness' or rumour-mongering. With homophobic bullying we also tend to find that boys rather than girls are more commonly both the perpetrators and the victims. Yet the sex of a young person as male or female does not predetermine whether they will engage in bullying or not. Instead it is the gendered expectations we place on boys and girls that determine this.

The expectations of femininity placed upon girls can mean that physical behaviour and direct aggression are discouraged as 'unladylike'. As a result less directly confrontational behaviour is common such as ostracism and gossip. For boys however physical aggression is a socially acceptable masculine trait and can be dismissed by educators as simply 'boys being boys'. When the roles are reversed with, for instance, girls exhibiting overt physical aggression and boys gossiping schools can stigmatise this behaviour as exceptionally problematic. In such situations our response to the bullying may not only denigrate what the bully did but also denigrate the perpetrator for not behaving as a 'typical girl' or 'typical boy'.

The pressure to conform to gender expectations can cause a great deal of anxiety amongst young people. Boys feel at a disadvantage if they are seen as weak or effeminate and girls risk exclusion or abuse if they do not invest in a 'feminine' appearance. This anxiety can lead to sexist and homophobic bullying. The stigma attached to being gay is not solely about the dislike of same-sex attraction but the fact that gay men are culturally aligned with femininity whilst lesbian women are culturally aligned with masculinity. Common homophobic insults additionally include those which imply or state that gay women are simply not 'attractive enough' to date men or boys are gay because they did not have a 'strong father figure'. In order to be a 'proper boy' or a 'proper girl' you must be heterosexual and act 'appropriately' for your gender.

This stigma around sexuality can be just as much about gender and sexism as it is about homophobia. It is important to recognise how these issues relate to one another so that both can be challenged. Once again, in settings where boys and girls are viewed as equals and the gender behaviours available to them are flexible and numerous you will find less homophobic bullying.

Box 3.1 Sex v Gender

Sex is often used to refer to the biological characteristics that define men and women. For example women have the physiology to bear children whilst men do not. **Gender** on the other hand is used to refer to socially constructed roles and attributes that a given society considers appropriate for boys or men and girls or women. Invariably features defining sex will be shared across different human societies whilst the defining features of gender differ greatly around the world. Some also draw the distinction that sex is biological whilst gender refers to the social groups of men and women, boys and girls.

The distinction between sex and gender is much contested and the above description is not prescriptive. It is important however to understand that the differences between the sexes and the behaviours deemed appropriate for them are not absolute or uninfluenced by cultural and social factors. Too often we use sex and gender to place a moral judgment on those who do not conform to our expectations.

Gender inequality

Inequality between the sexes has historically been justified by the myth that our anatomy determines our role in society and the belief that certain roles are of more social value. Women's physical capability to bear children is typically used to determine their role as primary caregiver. Women in the UK and USA do the majority of unpaid care for children and elderly relatives. In turn however this caring role is devalued and even penalised as each year a woman is absent from the workplace in the UK her future wages will reduce by four per cent (Olsen and Welby, 2004).

Heterosexual and gay men who are seen to reject the masculine gender roles deemed appropriate to their sex can experience this discrimination too. Both are seen as feminine and to be a woman is culturally degraded. Similarly heterosexual and lesbian women who adopt traits deemed masculine are often viewed as 'unnatural' and threatening.

Age

Homophobic bullying can be perpetrated by people of all ages. We tend to associate the problem with pupils in secondary school. It can begin in our primary or elementary schools however and continue into college, university or the workplace. Pupils who continue to perpetrate homophobic abuse after school are likely to be penalised: losing jobs, positions at university or even finding themselves guilty of prejudice-based crime (hate crime). It is important therefore that this behaviour is challenged as early as possible.

It is only recently that the importance of addressing homophobic bullying in primary school has been embraced. I had a primary school teacher say to me at a conference at which I had been invited to speak about challenging homophobic bullying in primary and secondary schools that she thought that this topic was 'Really more a big school issue…' When a teacher describes secondary school as big school (presumably she refers to her primary school as 'small school' or 'little school'?) we can see easily why we so often end up placing a sticking plaster over the symptoms of homophobia in our high schools: expressly because too few of our primary or elementary school colleagues recognise the vital role they play in educating children (and each other) about the need to introduce children to an awareness of different families, children's various home circumstances and to look at diversity through more than simply the lens of race, ethnicity or disability.

Whilst Years 7 to 11 (Grades 6 to 10) are those where we see homophobic bullying, it tends to decrease in sixth form (Grades 11 and 12). More people are openly gay here – and it is interesting to note that teachers tell me regularly that pupils who are 'out' will frequently experience less bullying than their peers whom others perceive as gay. I have also found that gay and lesbian teachers in sixth form settings are more likely to be 'out' to their A-level students. Interestingly, this is tacitly appealing to their sixth formers' maturity not to blab to the younger years the fact that they are gay. Years 7 to 11 (Grades 6 to 10) often remain in blissful ignorance of gay or lesbian teachers in their school and therefore we see a dearth of thriving, successful, positive 'out' gay role models in the teaching profession.

Disability

The experiences of pupils with disabilities or additional needs can often be overlooked and EACH, the Anti-Bullying Alliance, Bullying Inervention Group and similar organizations regularly receives enquiries from teachers (seeking support or staff training) who work with pupils with additional needs. Pupils with, for example, autism or Asperger's can fail to recognise the impact homophobic classroom insults can have on their peers. Sometimes pupils will simply be expressing legitimate curiosity about differences but without the understanding to utilise appropriate language. Most insults are brought in from home and elder siblings but teachers often express exasperation at how racist or homophobic parents can be which makes educating children with additional needs that much harder. Other times pupils may be lashing out at others and targeting differences as an expression of personal frustration.

It is important to remember that, of course, post-pubertal pupils with additional needs have a sexuality just as mainstream school youngsters do. Teachers often voice concerns to EACH as to whether they are granting enough attention to the pupils in their school who may be struggling to understand or come to terms with their evolving sexuality – especially when this is gay. It is essential to bear in mind also that a significant minority of young people with additional needs will also be gay.

Ethnicity

Everyone has an 'ethnicity' and shares common national or cultural traditions with others. In England and Wales the majority of the population is White British. However we also have a rich cultural history of ethnic diversity with a large White Irish, Asian British, Black African and Black Caribbean population as well as many people from across Europe, the Middle East and the Americas (ONS, 2011). Many will share multiple and sometimes conflicting national or cultural traditions depending on their ethnicity. This can be particularly evident in young people who will have lived in the UK all their life but whose parents or grandparents grew up outside of it.

Whilst it is important not to stereotype any group we must recognise that views on sexual orientation and gender identity will vary and mean different things within different cultures. Whilst some cultures celebrate and revere diversity of sexuality and gender identity there are many which are not as inclusive or tolerant (see Box 3.2). For young people who come from, or whose parents come from, countries where being gay is considered 'deviant' their attitude towards same-sex relationships will be more conservative than those from countries which value same-sex relationships.

Box 3.2 Being gay around the world

Dozens of countries around the world continue to outlaw same-sex relationships and prosecute people for being gay. In Iran, Mauritania, Saudi Arabia, Sudan and Yemen being gay is punishable with the death penalty and in many others gay and lesbian people face imprisonment. Even in nations where same-sex relationships are not illegal lesbian and gay people are still denied equal rights and experience unequal ages of consent or marriage bans.

The UK, and to an extent the United States, often prides itself on its progressive track record (particularly in the last decade) towards equal rights for lesbian and gay people. It should not be forgotten however that anti-gay laws in countries such as India and many African nations are the legacy of British colonial rule.

Coming from a family background with strong views against same-sex people can lead pupils to engage in homophobic bullying. If a young person has been taught that same-sex relationships are wrong they may express this through bullying behaviours which target anyone who is or is perceived to be gay. These young people can also struggle with intense internalised homophobia if they are gay. Whilst positive visibility within the media, education and wider society is poor for all gay people it is exceptionally lacking for those from an ethnic minority background. As a result there is a commonly held misconception that all gay young people are white.

This can lead us to overlook the experiences of those from different ethnicities and even anticipate or ignore homophobia because of their cultural background.

Regardless of ethnicity or cultural background there are plenty of adults who hold onto archaic prejudices and pass these on to their children. When a person's justification for their prejudice is related to their national or cultural identity educators can feel less confident about challenging these attitudes. After all it is easier to challenge someone with whom you perceive a shared national or cultural tradition than it is to challenge someone whose culture you know or understand little about. Despite this there is a strong legal and moral imperative for us all to challenge homophobia whenever it occurs just as there is an imperative to challenge racism wherever this occurs. Whilst these issues may sometimes seem in conflict they should be considered in unison. Respect for equality and diversity does not work if it is applied only to one 'issue' or constituency of interest. Educating young people about respecting and celebrating our national or cultural differences can be a great platform for recognising and celebrating all kinds of different families, relationships and so on. After all respect, empathy and kindness are transferable skills.

Faith

In many ways the homophobic attitudes manifested by some with strong religious convictions look largely similar to those whose national identity is used as a justification for their prejudice. The value that different nations place on sexual orientation and gender identity is often underpinned by religious belief and religion shapes many cultures around the world.

Religion can be a divisive topic particularly when discussed in relation to sexuality. For some religion is about peace, love, dialogue and community whilst for others it calls to mind sectarianism, war, hate and narrow-mindedness. Faith is frequently used as a justification for homophobic prejudice as evidenced by recent debates on same-sex marriage in the UK and USA. As a result, discussions of lesbian and gay equality and religious freedom can often be seen to be in competition with one another.

Religion encompasses a multitude of beliefs however and is not synonymous with homophobic prejudice. The author Symon Hill notes for any tie between religion and oppression there is an equal tie between religion and liberty (Hill, 2010).

Great Britain is today a largely secular society. Although Christianity remains its largest religion, fewer and fewer people are identifying themselves as Christian each census. At the same time, with immigration, there has been a rise in the number of people identifying as Muslim, Buddhist, Hindu or Jewish and a quarter of the population in England and Wales report having no religion (ONS, 2011). Great Britain is not however a secular state and religion still plays an important part in our school system. In England around a third of all state-funded schools are those 'with a religious character' (DfE, 2010). The vast majority are Church of England and schools 'with a religious character' also include Roman Catholic, Jewish, Muslim and Greek Orthodox amongst other religions.

The role of religion within the British school system is not without controversy. People of all faiths and no faith are critical of religious schools' right to discriminate in selection and recruitment to favour pupils from a particular religious background. In 2014 a number of Muslim majority schools in Birmingham, United Kingdom, were embroiled in four separate investigations examining claims that hard-line Islamists were 'trying to take control'. The investigations into alleged extremism in some Birmingham schools were sparked by allegations of gender discrimination, homophobia, extremist views, bullying and unfair employment practices.

Similar concerns were raised in 2012 when Catholic schools were found to be distributing a pamphlet entitled 'Pure Manhood: How to become the man God wants you to be' which featured homophobic commentary and undermined HIV prevention campaigns. Further controversy followed later in the year when the Catholic Education Service wrote to all state-funded Roman Catholic secondary schools in England and Wales highlighting that it was every Catholic's duty to oppose equal marriage for lesbian and gay people.

Cases such as these and its accompanying media frenzy undermine public trust in schools with a religious character and their ability to promote a safe learning environment for all. The Department for Education said it takes action if there are any concerns that a school is not meeting the independent schools' standards. Of course, some faith schools will be liberal in their attitude to equality and diversity whilst others will be at the other end of any continuum. What is important as far as any pupil is concerned is that religious convictions do not allow, foster or promulgate bullying of any kind and prejudice-based bullying is a type which can too easily thrive in extreme circumstances.

There are fortunately many examples of schools with a religious character, or serving a largely religious constituency, fostering a deep commitment to equality, civil rights and the promotion of mutual understanding. EACH and other similar organizations has worked with many faith schools, as well as religious young people, to prevent homophobic bullying within their settings. These schools and their pupils feel that the use of religion to justify homophobic oppression belittles their faith and they possess a conviction to challenge this, and do so for instance through films for schools they have produced with the charity.

Indeed, EACH consulted closely with the Church of England, its staff and ministers in the lead up to its creation of *Valuing All God's Children: Guidance for Church of England Schools on Challenging Homophobic Bullying* (Church of England Archbishops Council Education Division, 2014). This is a major step forward in the Church's efforts to reconcile differences held by some in its congregation endorsing same-sex relationships on the one hand and condemning homophobic bullying on the other.

Religious Education (RE) has an important role to play in promoting social cohesion and the values of respect and empathy. Ofsted has argued however that the full potential of RE is not being realised in many schools (Ofsted, 2013). Effective RE places enquiry at the heart of learning, engages pupils in 'big questions', enables them to reconsider their positions, investigate religions and explore new possibilities (Ofsted, 2013). RE provides a great opportunity to teach pupils about a range of religious and cultural perspectives surrounding matters of sexual diversity, gender and challenge some taken-for-granted assumptions.

In Chapter 4 I explore some of these taken-for-granted assumptions and develop a broader understanding of the beliefs that underlie homophobic bullying and how some young people attempt to justify this behaviour.

Key points

- Homophobic bullying should be challenged from primary school.

- Perpetrators of homophobic bullying can be heterosexual, lesbian, gay, bisexual or simply unsure of their sexuality.

- Be wary of reinforcing gender stereotypes when challenging homophobic bullying.

- Anti-homophobic bullying work complements wider equality and diversity work challenging racist, faith-based, disablist and other prejudice-based bullying.

- Religious convictions should in no circumstances be used as a justification for allowing or excusing homophobic bullying.

CHAPTER 4

Why Do Young People Bully Homophobically?

EACH has worked with over 10,000 young people to date exploring their experiences and understanding of homophobia, transphobia, sexism and cyberbullying. Targets, bystanders and perpetrators have engaged with EACH's services over the years. Listening to the wide-ranging voices of young people has led to a broad understanding of the reasons young people bully homophobically. Some common justifications and scenarios are explored in detail below.

> 'Gay people make me uncomfortable and I don't want them near me.' Lincoln, 16

Whilst views such as this are now in the minority, the fact remains that many people still believe that lesbian, gay and bisexual people are 'wrong', 'unnatural' or do not deserve equal rights. These sentiments can too easily be echoed by others especially when lack of life experience or a limited exposure to diversity in the wider world has allowed them to form negative assumptions about gay people. It is important to bear in mind the distinction between gay people being 'invisible' and being 'absent'. Gay people are ever present but rendered invisible by language, advertising, television, film and magazine portrayals. If you are not depicted you are, by default, voiceless, powerless, worthless. You only matter if you are counted and you are only counted if you matter. It is a self-fulfilling prophecy.

Prejudice usually involves viewing people as part of a group and assuming that everyone in this group is the same. People of all ages can have a very limited view of what gay people are really like – which is in reality extraordinarily like everyone else. Young people hear about gay issues from a variety of sources including family, friends and the media. All too often though myths and stereotypes abound – based on overheard ridiculing expressed by adults, older teenagers and elder siblings. Lack of life experience or exposure to diversity simply compounds ignorance and misinformation.

The coverage of England's equal marriage debate in 2013 illustrates this point. The media frequently gave voice to the views of those who compared same-sex marriage to incest and bestiality. We cannot take it for granted that young people will question these assertions and understand the dangers inherent within such opinions. Educators must engage proactively with topical debates such as same-sex marriage if they are to prevent young people from rehearsing these views and targeting their peers.

It is vitally important therefore that teachers and staff in all schools address issues of sexual diversity with pupils in their classes because the school system is a microcosm of society at large. Children need to be exposed to many different beliefs and opinions. Schools have the opportunity, and in fact the obligation, to prepare them for the outside world where they will work with sexually diverse men and women. Pupils must be prepared to enter society with a more open mind, where all individuals deserve the right to be who they are, regardless of sexual orientation.

> 'Anyone can be called gay. We say it to normal people just to insult them.' Janine, 14

Whilst of course, not all young people or their teachers hold overtly homophobic views, some may unconsciously or otherwise maintain the belief that being heterosexual is 'normal' and right whilst being gay is inferior and less acceptable. Once again this attitude is consistently reinforced through mainstream films, TV shows, advertising and magazines where being gay is represented as a source of anxiety, a threat, an object of amusement or abuse, or simply not represented at all.

So, who has the problem? Teachers, especially those with strong religious convictions, struggling with 'out' gay teens but happy to see gay people on *Strictly Come Dancing* or any number of game, chat or reality shows? The fact is that, for many of our pupils, it is media portrayals exemplified by the diet of pseudo-psychological television programmes dressed up as 'science' such as *Queer Eye for the Straight Guy* that are informing how many see gay people and particularly gay men (see Box 4.1).

> **Box 4.1** Reality television shows exacerbating or exploding myths about gay men's 'lifestyle'
>
> **Queer Eye for the Straight Guy**
>
> Five gay men who specialise in fashion, food and wine, grooming, culture, and interior design go to the rescue of hapless heterosexual men with no sense of fashion or anything else and complete a makeover. The contestant is often a man who cannot cook, is culturally unsophisticated and oblivious about home décor. The hosts show the heterosexual man their perceptions of how to fix these problems pertaining to their corresponding specialisms.
>
> The show led to a spin-off in the USA entitled *Queer Eye For The Straight Girl*. Following the format of the original show the new series focussed on makeovers for women. The hosts were called 'The Gal Pals' and included three gay men and a lesbian. The show was unsuccessful and lasted only one series.
>
> **Playing It Straight**
>
> This was a reality show in which one woman spent time on a ranch with a selection of men in an attempt to distinguish those who were *gay* from those who were *heterosexual*. All of the gay men pretended to be heterosexual. In addition to engaging in group activities with the men the woman went on individual dates with them. Over the course of the episodes the female contestant voted to eliminate the men she believed to be gay. At the end of the show the woman chose one man. If he was heterosexual the man and woman split the prize money, but if

he was gay he received all the money. The show also aired in the Netherlands as *Herken De Homo* (*Find The Gay One*).

Boy Meets Boy

A gay man is tasked with choosing a partner from a group of 15 potential male suitors. The show featured the twist that the 'leading man' did not know that the mix of suitors included both gay and heterosexual men.

Seriously, Dude, I'm Gay

A reality special which Fox planned to broadcast on 7 June, 2004. The two-hour special featured two heterosexual men competing to pass as gay for a week. If the contestants were able to convince their friends and family that they were actually gay they would win a $50,000 dollar prize. At its conclusion a panel of gay men, who believe one of the contestants to be gay, would select the winner.

Whilst lesbian women are increasingly indivisible from their heterosexual peers the presentation of gay men in certain television situations even today harks back to their portrayal in 1970s situation comedies like *It Ain't Half Hot Mum* and *Are You Being Served?* The comedy series *Little Britain*'s Daffyd is the modern incarnation of Clarence, Dick Emery's 1970s effeminate gay male character who regularly chirruped 'Hello, Honky Tonks!' whilst his character Mandy's catchphrase became the nation's comic catchphrase for a decade: 'Ooh, you are awful – but I like you!'

As Alan J. Woodward observes in *Dick Emery's Comedy Characters: Confusing the Polarity* (Woodward, 2014):

> Clarence, also known as 'Honky Tonks', had actually been in Dick Emery's act for many years in one guise or another although he admitted that it was the one character that had undergone the biggest change. When Clarence began life homosexuality was only hinted [at] in terms of comedy rather than brought straight out into the open. In the main these characters were more familiar to cabaret than TV. Emery

stated that adopting a camp attitude was a useful ploy when faced with an unresponsive audience staring across their plate of steak and chips blankly at a performer. 'Why the suggestion of homosexuality should be funny is imponderable – perhaps our laughter is defence, a reaction against hidden fears about our innermost tendencies', he contemplated. By the 1970s gay characters appeared more openly although they were portrayed as farcical and camp and created purely for comic relief. At the same time as Clarence became a staple of Emery's repertoire, John Inman was starring on television as Grace Brothers' decidedly effeminate (but undeclared homosexual [sic]) menswear salesman Mr. Humphrey's in *Are You Being Served?*, and Larry Grayson was making a name for himself camping it up as the comedian with a decidedly gay persona which actually formed the mainstay of his act. Prior to the 1970s Clarence had appeared with heavy make-up; he also wore a wig of short, blonde, swept-back hair. However, in the early part of the decade men began to wear brighter and more adventurous clothes and Clarence soon found that he was being outdone. So out went the old props and in came a more fashion conscious character complete with outrageous outfits, accessories and a far more effeminate manner. Clarence was probably the template for *Little Britain*'s Daffyd and one imagines that Matt Lucas has taken the character and shown us his modern day version. In the early 1970s, Clarence was the only gay in the village.

Interviewer: Excuse me, sir.

Clarence: Oh, hello Honky Tonks, how are you?

Interviewer: I'm asking questions about class distinction.

Clarence: Oh, yes?

Interviewer: Do you believe there's an 'us' and a 'them'?

Clarence: Well, it doesn't bother me really – I'm one of those!

Box 4.2 contains a useful activity for exploring lesbian and gay stereotypes with your pupils. Although young people who hold on to stereotypes may not wish to withhold equal rights from gay people they may well have their sense of who gay men and women 'are' skewed by television depictions and not see it as a priority or empathise with the issue. As a result they can unknowingly perpetrate it themselves through taunting which they will call 'banter' or be complicit bystanders when name-calling turns into homophobic bullying.

The belief that being gay is inferior to being heterosexual leads to subtle behaviours such as jokes and vocabulary that can be very damaging to gay young people. One of the most obvious examples is the pejorative use of the word 'gay' amongst young people to describe something as worthless, wrong, dull, stupid or inferior. This use of language does not always constitute homophobic bullying as it is often targeted at objects and situations rather than individuals. It does however function as a micro-aggression which elevates heterosexuality above lesbian, gay and bisexual identities making the latter synonymous with the dysfunctional, the inept and the undesirable (Aiden et al., 2013). It is this belief, held by some, that, particularly, gay people are dysfunctional, unstable and contaminated (either mentally or physically) that feeds into many of the arguments for not granting equal rights and if we continue to let these attitudes go unchallenged we risk damaging irrevocably the self-esteem and self-worth of, particularly gay young people. The USA still has much ground to make up to be on an equal footing with legislation and attitudes in the UK. GLSEN must envy the legislation and attitudes enjoyed in the United Kingdom on gay and transgender equality and does a sterling job in challenging anti-gay bullying in the USA.

Box 4.2 Gay visibility activity

Divide the class into small groups and ask each group to think of a famous gay person or character. On sticky notes they then write down traits of this person or character. After 5–10 minutes invite pupils to feed back on the gay figure they were discussing and the traits they identified. Record the pupils' thoughts on the board and ask them to consider whether any of these traits are common to all gay people or to people in general.

Explain that people can sometimes assume that all gay people are alike, for example that all gay men have great dress sense or all lesbians are butch. Highlight that these beliefs are stereotypes that are oversimplified, frequently untrue and can be very offensive.

Ask the pupils to identify any further stereotypes about gay people and discuss:

- Where do we see/hear these stereotypes portrayed – for example in the news, on TV, in films or at school?

- What do the stereotypes have in common?

- Are any of the stereotypes funny? If so, why?

- How are these stereotypes dangerous or damaging?

- How do stereotypes affect the way we behave?

- How can these stereotypes be challenged?

Explain that stereotypes lead to prejudice and discrimination. The assumption that all gay people are alike leads to prejudging gay people. It can also mean that the many gay people who do not fit these stereotypes feel invisible and voiceless.

Adapted from EACH (2014)

The subtle reinforcement of heterosexual privilege does not start and end however with 'That's so gay'. There are numerous ways in which the experiences of gay young people can be trivialised and ridiculed. Even the very words lesbian, gay and bisexual can be deployed as a cheap joke or insult. If pupils and indeed their teachers cannot adopt appropriate language without embarrassment it is problematic for creating an inclusive school culture. Once educators begin to have age-appropriate and open discussions with pupils about sexual diversity pupils will be better prepared to discuss these topics appropriately and maturely. A prevailing issue concerning discussing sexual diversity is the frequently conservative approach to sex and relationship education (SRE) adopted by schools. Same-sex relationships are rarely discussed which not only puts the health and wellbeing of gay pupils at risk but reinforces heterosexual privilege. As pupils become more exposed to gay relationships within wider society questions about this aspect of gay lives will naturally arise. Yet too often the information to which pupils have access is inaccurate or generalised. This can lead to same-sex relationships becoming a source of mockery or derision. Once again inclusive and age-appropriate conversations about same-sex relationships in SRE will reinforce just how ordinary and everyday it is to be gay.

> 'I called someone gay for cowering out of a challenge during a football match.' Carl, 15

Many of our beliefs about what is normal and desirable are informed by gender and the way that certain behaviours, characteristics and qualities are culturally aligned with being a man or being a woman. As part of its Reach project, EACH worked with groups of young people exploring gender stereotyping and the pressures that they feel as boys or girls. The young people felt that girls are often judged by what they look like and wear whilst boys are often expected to be strong and interested in sport. It was also felt that when girls are interested in activities that boys are 'supposed to like' and boys are interested in activities girls are 'supposed to like' they can become the target of bullying.

Young people can feel the pressure to conform to these gendered ideas from a very young age in order to fit in and be popular. A report by the NSPCC in 2013 found that young people aged between 10 and 12 years of age spoke of feeling they were 'being pushed' into being a 'particular kind of "girl" or "boy"' (Renold and Tetlow, 2013).

From an early age friendships between boys and girls are subject to romantic innuendo and platonic opposite sex relationships can become stigmatised (Renold and Tetlow, 2013). The investment in boyfriend-girlfriend culture starts in primary school becoming a way in which children and young people establish and maintain status. In order to maintain this status boys often feel they should define themselves in opposition to 'girls, feminine behaviour and gay or bisexual men' whilst girls feel they should define themselves in opposition to 'boys, masculine behaviour and lesbian or bisexual women' (Aiden *et al.*, 2013, p.15). This can lead to homophobic or sexist abuse as young people seek to belittle behaviour that does not conform to their ideas of gender in order to assert their identity as a boy or a girl. In settings with decreasing incidents of homophobia one will often find an increase in the gendered behaviours open to boys and girls and more freedom of expression.

> 'Lesbian, gay and bisexual issues were only ever mentioned once in our school.' Nadyia, 17

Schools will very rarely endorse overtly homophobic behaviour and clear legislation should be in place to safeguard against this. Staff both in schools and other settings can nevertheless be complicit in reinforcing attitudes about the superiority of heterosexuality and gender conformity by rendering gay people invisible. Even where anti-bullying policies are in place (and individual incidents reported and dealt with) educational settings will struggle to challenge homophobic bullying effectively if underlying attitudes go unchallenged through preventative measures (Aiden *et al.*, 2013). Whilst great work is being done to address homophobic bullying in many schools, they often shy away from engaging young people in constructive and age-appropriate conversation about sexuality and instead treat it solely as a discipline issue.

It is not a surprise that schools are reluctant to discuss these issues with their pupils when for 15 years they were actively discouraged from doing so. Section 28 of the Local Government Act 1988 was one of the most pernicious pieces of anti-gay legislation in Britain: prohibiting local authorities from 'promoting the teaching in any maintained school of the acceptability of homosexuality as a pretended family relationship'. Since its repeal came into effect in England on 18 November 2003 we have seen a raft of legislative changes advancing the rights of lesbian, gay and bisexual people. From workplace protections, fostering and adoption rights, the introduction of civil partnerships to, in 2014, the introduction of same-sex marriage – no longer can the relationships of lesbian, gay or bisexual people be dismissed as 'pretend', 'unacceptable' or illegitimate.

Whilst we might try to ameliorate the effects of bigotry in our schools, some pupils come from homes which impart ignorance or intolerance. Other households do not foster openness and acceptance and many pupils come from homes where children and their parents have not been exposed to other cultures or minority groups. Some parents choose not to expose their children to diversity and others live in communities which lack a great deal of diversity. School may be the only place where these pupils are exposed to cultures and people who are different from them.

If my years of supporting schools in challenging homophobia has taught me anything it is that the cast of Section 28's shadow did not end in the year of its repeal in 2003. Although Section 28 was not even targeted at schools per se, many teachers are still too unconfident, too overworked and sometimes too misinformed to address matters of sexual orientation beyond actual bullying matters. In summer 2013 45 academies across Britain came under scrutiny as it was revealed that their sex and relationship education (SRE) policies included outdated Section 28-esque statements prohibiting the 'promotion of homosexuality'. This fear of 'promoting' lesbian, gay and bisexual issues has permeated school cultures for decades, effectively silencing constructive discussion about sexuality between pupils and teachers. As I have said previously, all too often addressing this topic comes down to a brave, sole teacher who has picked up the issue because they have someone in their personal life who is gay, they identify as gay themselves or they are attempting to support a gay pupil. Over the years I have considered often how many lesbian or gay teachers have entered the profession to 'make a difference' for the pupils in their schools, colleagues and ultimately society beyond imparting their subject matter knowledge. The fact that so many gay teachers feel affirmed only to be out to their colleagues or sixth formers says much about how confident they are in 2015 to be their authentic, fully-rounded selves to everyone in their school: a privilege enjoyed by heterosexual teachers daily. This quote is from a male teacher in Blaenau Gwent when I was delivering a staff training input at his school:

> 'I'd rather my 15-year-old son came home and told me he'd raped or murdered someone than told me he was gay.'

Yes, he was appropriately disciplined.

In 2009 EACH was awarded Big Lottery funding to work with lesbian, gay, bisexual, transgender and heterosexual young people in order to challenge prejudice-based bullying. The five-year grant for EACH's Reach project enabled the charity to work with young people across Bristol, South Gloucestershire and North Somerset to create a practical toolkit for teachers and putting young people's voices at the heart of work challenging homophobic, sexist and cyberbullying. You may think it difficult to find fault with such an investment. The announcement of this funding in August 2009 however was denounced by the then leader of the Bristol Tories, Councillor Richard Eddy, as a 'mistaken and misguided, outrageous waste of money' (Webster, 2009). The criticism was buoyed by a front page spread from the Bristol Evening Post asking 'So you call this equality?' (Webster, 2009). Both challenged the award for funding a minority issue and singling out gay young people for 'special treatment' (Webster, 2009).

The so-called 'privileging' of minority groups for preferential treatment is a common criticism waged against equalities initiatives. What critics ignore is that those in the majority enjoy an invisible, privileged social status on a daily basis. This privilege freely rewards those in the majority with health, education, safety, security, recognition and numerous basic rights. For those in the minority such rights are hard won. Too often gay young people are denied the opportunity to thrive, realise their academic and social potential and engage positively in all aspects of life. It is for this reason that EACH set about working with local lesbian, gay, bisexual, transgender *and* heterosexual young people on initiatives which strive to build confidence in the very institutions set up to nurture them.

> 'Reach has been so beneficial to me in personal and practical ways. It helped me voice views I once felt were unheard and allowed my voice to help others by challenging homophobic and transphobic language and bullying. Winning the Diana Award in 2013 felt amazing – like others were not only recognising my voice but the voice of many other lesbian, gay, bisexual and transgender young people.' Travis, 18

By 2014 EACH had worked with 3500 young people and created the *Reach Teaching Resource: A Practical Toolkit for Challenging Homophobic, Sexist and Cyberbullying.* Designed in close consultation with young people the toolkit supports teachers to open up a dialogue with their pupils around homophobia, sexism and cyberbullying and reflect upon pupils' experiences, values and existing knowledge to meaningfully challenge prejudice-based bullying (EACH, 2014).

What we find when we do have constructive and age-appropriate conversations with young people is that they share a greater understanding of rights, respect and equality than we give them justice. These allow them to express their views on what it means to be lesbian, gay or bisexual in society today. Young people recognise that whilst great progress has been made the terrible oppression suffered by gay people is part of our recent history and we are still not all equal. We still live in a society where:

- one in four gay or transgender young people have been assaulted and one in two have received threats because of their sexuality (METRO Youth Chances, 2014)

- such abuse is portrayed as an inevitability of gay lives rather than a symptom of others' ignorance and prejudice

- support and guidance has to be sought out by gay young people rather than offered. Phrases such as 'that's so gay' reinforce feelings of isolation, insecurity and hostility on a daily basis.

It is understandable that many teachers do not see this issue as a key responsibility when the teaching of equality, same-sex relationships and prejudice has little to no space in the national curriculum. Personal social health and economic (PSHE) education remains a non-statutory subject, as does SRE. In addition the guidance for SRE has not been updated since 2000 pre-dating the Sexual Offences Act 2003, the repeal of Section 28 and the 2010 Equalities legislation. SRE was only updated voluntarily in the United Kingdom in 2014 by a voluntary sector conglomerate led by the PSHE Association (Brooks, 2014). Even Ofsted recognises that schools are not doing enough to ensure pupils have a good awareness and understanding of all forms of diversity and discrimination, highlighting specifically homophobia as a weak point (Ofsted, 2012). Schools have been tasked with the paradox of combating homophobia without ever actually being supported to talk about the root of the problem.

Building on this, there is still a Government impetus for schools to put in place strategies to improve their ability to challenge homophobic bullying and consulting with EACH or other training organisations can help you here. On 5 April 2011 the public sector equality duty came into force in England, Scotland and Wales as part of the Equality Act 2010. It requires that public bodies – including state, academy and free schools – must 'consider all individuals when carrying out their day-to-day work – in shaping policy, in delivering services and in relation to their own employees' (c.149). Schools whose policies and practices are seen to discriminate against or disadvantage members of the pupil body are vulnerable to complaints of unlawful treatment. If schools are to truly challenge homophobic bullying they must also reflect on their own practices and attitudes in order to assess whether they are subtly reinforcing this prejudice on a daily basis. We return to this later.

Key points

- Schools may be the only place where children and young people are having prejudiced views challenged.

- Homophobia can be enforced through our collective subtle behaviours and innuendo that communicate powerful messages to lesbian, gay, bisexual and heterosexual young people.

- We cannot challenge homophobia without challenging the assumptions about gender which underline this behaviour.

- Silence can send the loudest message about the value placed on lesbian, gay and bisexual identities.

CHAPTER 5

What is the Impact on Those Being Bullied?

Homophobic bullying can affect a pupil's emotional and social wellbeing not to mention their physical health. They are likely to remove themselves from social interactions in class and other activities previously enjoyed. You are likely to witness their seemingly inexplicable slump in grades and whole-day or 'in school' truancy. They are 'there' but not attending all their lessons to avoid their tormentors and even if in class physically they are definitely not 'there' in terms of concentrating on the lesson. Ultimately you may observe their departure from your school early or a move to a different school. The severity of the effects on a pupil depends entirely on the individual, their resilience and coping strategies. Inconveniently for us, pupils are unlikely to respond to homophobic bullying in the same way. We and the schools in which we work however have a legal, ethical and moral obligation to provide equal access to education and equal protection under the law for all students.

For many sexual minority students schools are unsafe, and survival – not education – is the priority (Weiler, 2003, p.10).

Box 5.1 Homophobic bullying in the UK

Youth Chances (METRO Youth Chances, 2014) is a social research project aiming to identify the needs of lesbian, gay, bisexual, transgender and questioning young people. Led by the charity Metro, the Youth Chances project conducted an online survey of 7000 young people aged 16 to 25 about their experiences of education, employment, health services, relationships and sexuality. The survey found that:

- three in four LGBT young people have experienced name-calling
- one in two LGBT young person has experienced harassment and threats
- one in four LGBT young person has experienced physical assault
- two in three LGBT young people felt their school supported its pupils badly in terms of sexual orientation and gender identity issues.

These negative experiences proved to have a devastating impact on the mental health and wellbeing of LGBT young people with:

- 52 per cent of respondents reporting having engaged in self-harm
- 42 per cent seeking medical help for anxiety or depression
- 44 per cent reporting thoughts of suicide.

Box 5.2 Homophobic bullying in the USA

The GLSEN 2011 *National School Climate Survey* report includes information from LGBT middle and high school students' experiences of homophobic language, harassment, discriminatory school practices and availability of support. The survey found that:

- 85 per cent of students heard gay used in a negative way (e.g. 'That's so gay') frequently or often in school

- 82 per cent were verbally harassed in the past year because of their sexual orientation

- 38 per cent experienced physical bullying because of their sexual orientation

- 55 per cent experienced homophobic cyberbullying

- the high incidence of harassment and assault is exacerbated by school staff who rarely, if ever, intervene on behalf of LGBT students

- 60 per cent of students who were harassed or assaulted in school did not report the incident to school staff most often believing little to no action would be taken or the situation could become worse if reported

- 36 per cent of the students who did report an incident said that school staff did nothing in response.

National surveys such as those conducted by Metro's Youth Chances project in the UK (Box 5.1) and GLSEN in the USA (Box 5.2) frequently indicate that homophobic bullying is prevalent. Teachers do not always recognise the homophobic bullying that occurs in their school and pupils do not always report the homophobic nature of the bullying they experience. Too many gay pupils today have precious few opportunities to acquire coping strategies or learn how to be resilient in the face of homophobic bullying or name-calling. We all know that bullying can cause severe and lasting damage to the self-esteem, wellbeing, happiness and potential of those who must endure it. EACH receives over 2000 support services calls and 4500 visits to its website annually from individuals seeking support around sexual orientation issues and gender identity matters. Most are from members of school staff, parents, grandparents or police officers seeking guidance on how best to deal with the homophobic bullying experienced by their children.

To gain an accurate snapshot of attitudes towards and experiences of homophobic bullying in your own setting it is useful to conduct an attitude survey to secure a broad understanding of your pupils' experiences. This does not have to be solely about homophobic bullying but can capture pupils' views about all forms of prejudice-based bullying. By undertaking an attitude survey you will be able to identify how homophobic, disablist, racist or sexist bullying manifests itself, the impact it has on your pupils and where these problems cross over. It may highlight, for example, that homophobic bullying is prevalent amongst pupils online yet they do not know how to report or respond to it. Gaining an insight into the experiences of your pupils will allow you to direct resources to address areas of need. Chapter 10 provides you with the types of question you can include in your own pupils' attitude surveys.

When I was at school and during my years in teaching, pupils who experienced homophobic bullying too often left at 16 years of age, exiting with qualifications much lower than their potential would have allowed them in happier circumstances. There is an historical link between bullying and low educational achievement as highlighted in numerous research reports on these issues. It is therefore logical to assume that the prevalence of homophobic bullying results in lesbian and gay pupils being especially disadvantaged when it comes to educational attainment. Conversely we are informed by Youth Chances's 2014 survey that 64 per cent of gay young people go on to university compared to 43 per cent of their heterosexual counterparts (METRO Youth Chances, 2014).

Although such statistics are not generalisable to all of the lesbian and gay population it does challenge the taken-for-granted assumption that lesbian and gay pupils are not achieving their full academic potential. It would be useful to know however which subjects these pupils go on to study at university and whether their academic choices are limited by their experiences at school. Little research has explored this to date. Further exploration into the experiences of gay people at university and in the workplace may continue to confirm what has for too long been the case that in commerce and industry gay people (particularly men) are more than likely to be 'in' at work compared with their peers in the service industry or arts. We know for instance, that there is a disproportionately far higher number of 'out' lesbian police officers in our Police Service than gay male officers.

Gay pupils frequently cite physical sports as the most feared activity within school but if we were to ask where the least feared space was to be found the library and study areas may reveal themselves as sites of refuge (Monk, 2011). What this tells us is that we are likely to find a higher representation of gay pupils in further and higher education compared to other equally valuable areas of work. To explore with any thoroughness the connection between sexual orientation and educational attainment would be impossible without also addressing issues of gender, socio-economic background, disability and race. The point here is that when young people are homophobically bullied it can impact upon them in varying ways (see Box 5.3) and low academic achievement is not the only signifier of distress. A school where any bullying is tolerated creates an unsafe learning and teaching environment for all.

Bullying feeds into a wider school culture of negativity which, as a visitor, one can perceive quite palpably. A school's governing body – regardless of whether the school is a local authority run state school, an academy, a free school or an independent boarding school – is subject to the Government's demands that schools make themselves safe places for each pupil, which means being safe from bullying.

Box 5.3 Types of responses to homophobic bullying

When young people are homophobically bullied they can respond in a number of ways:

- deny their sexuality either to themselves (if gay) or others who make reference to it

- develop low self-esteem and a negative self-image, lose self-confidence and limit their own aspirations

- project resentment onto other open or 'obvious' gay young people

- demonstrate feelings of anger (towards self and others), defensiveness, passive-aggression, shame or moroseness

- display self-ridicule to gain social acceptance (known as pro-behaviour)

- adopt risk-taking behaviours online and offline

- ideate or practise self-harm or suicide

- distrust others leading to isolation, loneliness, suspicion or paranoia

- experience changes in sleep patterns, appetite or health reported by parents or pupils

- display changes in attitude towards school and schooling including truanting from school or certain lessons.

Although it is a school's governors' legal responsibility to ensure this is happening it is the leadership team's ethical responsibility to effect this. It is important that all staff, at all levels, are aware of the school's approach to addressing all forms of bullying.

A life lived out of authenticity – in which lies are told to others (and even oneself) about who one 'is' – is at once emotionally exhausting and obstructive to any young person's, or indeed adult's, emotional and even physical development. Homophobia has a negative effect on the health and wellbeing of young people and of those around them. It can mean they internalise it as they negotiate their identities at school. Self-confidence can be severely undermined with homophobia directed inwards and manifesting itself as self-loathing.

Too many gay young people report feeling any number of negative emotions: anxious, 'stressed', worthless, ashamed, angry, isolated, fearful with feelings of incredible loneliness and a sense of abnormality. These emotions can lead to depression, self-harm, eating disorders or suicide attempts. It is well recognised that suicide and attempt-suicides are far more frequent in those young people who identify as gay than in the general youth population. The role of homophobic bullying in contributing to these negative emotions and mental health issues cannot be underestimated. As Box 5.4 highlights the connections between being bullied and suicide have been evidenced across the world.

Box 5.4 Bullying and Suicide: A Review, 2008

Suicide is the third leading cause of mortality in children and adolescents in the USA and around the world. During a review of 37 studies in 13 countries (including the USA, Canada, the UK, Germany, South Korea, Japan, South Africa) researchers at the Yale School of Medicine found connections between bullying, being bullied and suicide in children. The studies indicated that:

- bullying affects anywhere between 9 and 54 per cent of children

- bullying victims are two to nine times more likely to report suicidal thoughts than other children

- bullies also have an increased risk of suicidal behaviours.

In 2013 the UK counselling charity ChildLine recorded 837 reports of homophobic bullying from young people up to the age of 19 (NSPCC, 2014).

The most common problem cited by this group of young people was homophobic bullying. Fear of telling parents (or problems after telling them) was also a significant source of concern. Some young lesbian, gay, bisexual or transgender people reported being triply isolated, with schools, friends and families all being unsupportive at best or overtly homophobic at worst.

Some young people who were homophobically bullied reported being in a Catch-22 situation: by reporting the bullying to their school or parents they would effectively out themselves. Many were not yet prepared to do this often because of homophobic attitudes they had heard expressed by teachers and parents.

ChildLine counsellors report that young people calling about their sexual orientation are often extremely lonely and isolated and feel that they have nowhere else to turn.

In a lot of cases, says a counsellor, a young person doesn't call to talk about how to come out, they call to talk about the tremendous fear they feel about what will happen when he or she – but especially he – does come out, or gets found out.

NSPCC Information Service (personal
communication, 15 April 2014)

Recognising oneself as gay can manifest itself in a number of ways. Similarly coming out can follow a variety of permutations. Some people go into flat denial and attempt to fit in with their peers by dating or going out with the opposite sex to 'prove' they are heterosexual. Others are aggressively homophobic to distance themselves from 'accusations of gayness'. Most gay young people however come out either to a trusted friend, a favourite teacher, a youth worker (or similar), a sibling or, not uncommonly, a grandparent. This often takes a great deal of thought and reflection because there is the possibility of losing close friends and being disowned by family. The latter is a horrifying prospect for almost all young people.

Most older gay adults have grown up believing that their sexuality is something of which to be more or less ashamed and that in many circumstances they must hide it. The younger the adult, the less likely they are to feel this except where religion or culture confers powerful early messages about same-sex relationships in a negative way. Whilst much older gay people will have heard themselves and others referred to directly and indirectly as queers, fairies, poofters, dykes and the like they are less likely to have heard insults in the classroom. There was a time when, although derided, gay or lesbian people were sneered at in spiteful lowered tones as 'one of them' but the issue was not one heard in their classroom. Today's generation of young people, on the other hand, are the ones to be aware of their sexual orientation and arguably the most well adjusted to it. Ironically it is also the generation to have heard 'That's so gay!' most frequently deployed as a put-down, insult or derogatory remark. Whenever 'gay' is used inappropriately it means variously pathetic, dull, unfashionable, idiotic, ridiculous, stupid, uncool, boring, broken, ridiculous, naff, crazy and so on. It is vital to acknowledge here that each adjective is a deleterious one conveying a powerful sense that whatever it is being applied to is without value or worth: undesirable, less-than, objectionable or negative.

There are myriad reasons why gay men and women, now in their 40s or older, did not come out whilst at school. Most were fearful of censure, rejection and, for some, violence from classmates or family members. Some cultures are incredibly and actively hostile towards gay and lesbian people and their relationships. The pressure on young gay men and women who live in these cultures to marry is huge. It is true that some do not even realise they are gay thanks to a lack of positive role models and the portrayal of heterosexuality still widely prevalent in society created by television, films, books and advertising, particularly for black and minority ethnic young people.

It is actually quite surprising how many men and women have the courage not to marry, such is the pressure on us all to do so. From the time we first kiss someone of the opposite sex aged four, in a playground or at a children's party, our parents, grandparents and friends of parents are delighted and often proceed to reinforce the absolute 'when you grow up and get married' at any given opportunity. Today, Britain is a nation of mostly secular, white British people for whom religion does not exert an undue influence on whether a young gay man or woman decides to come out and later go on to marry someone of the same sex. Many other men and women however feel obliged to marry someone of the opposite sex despite knowing full well they are incompatible. There is research to be undertaken to establish how married lesbian women negotiate their predicament but their gay male counterparts either go on to have clandestine sexual assignations with other men facilitated by geo-social apps on their smartphone, surreptitiously visit public sex environments (woodlands or restrooms) or live an isolated life, out of authenticity, where their sexuality and therefore true identity is soul-destroyingly subjugated. It is certainly true that many more divorced men and women are going on to enter same-sex relationships than ever before whilst more people whose spouses have died are entering same-sex relationships similarly. Some leave their spouse when their children leave home.

Identifying publicly as lesbian, gay or bisexual can be a very traumatic experience for anyone regardless of social class, age or the level of support from family. For a sizeable minority staying in the closet feels safer than risking social and workplace ostracism. Coming out as gay at school can mean having precious few people to whom to turn for advice and help when it is needed.

Whether gay pupils are out or 'in' there is a sense of guilt. Everyone, whether we care to admit it or not, has a deep-seated desire to be 'approved of'. Gay young people long to be accepted for who they are and are too often at risk of searching everywhere to find that acceptance. If they are 'in the closet' they experience a variety of emotions. Closeted gay youngsters feel guilty for not being honest with their families, their friends and themselves. Not having anyone to turn to for guidance and advice can be a debilitating and very lonely experience. That feeling of aloneness is why gay young people make unsafe decisions and risk-take, often into and throughout adulthood.

One of the issues with which EACH and other training providers has always grappled is negotiating a course between the need to illustrate to adults (with responsibility to support young people who come out) why homophobic bullying must be challenged, on the one hand, and not being seen to pathologise gay young people by over-emphasising the negatives of being young and gay on the other. Agencies, research findings or individuals who shroud-wave, constantly portraying gay young people's existence in terms of mental health issues and pathologising their experience of coming out, do no one any favours.

Homophobia will only end when society catches up with the laws we have passed to protect gay people and create safe and equal places of work and study. Then we can stop placing emphasis on what goes wrong for gay young people (and subsequently adults) when we fail to meet their needs.

Society is predominantly heterosexual and gay people are reminded of this fact on a daily basis. As I type this chapter I am heartened to see the NatWest Bank in the UK running a television commercial featuring female twins, one of whom has a girlfriend whilst the other a boyfriend – very low key, no nonsense, a truly excellent way of portraying gay people in advertising and a commendable move by NatWest. Lloyds Bank, also in the UK, previously ran a positive campaign in one of its leaflets and in a television commercial featuring a same-sex male couple in cartoon format. Unilever currently has a commercial running as part of its 'Cupidity' range in its efforts to sell Cornetto ice-cream (Unilever, 2014). The advertisement portrays a same-sex lesbian couple's burgeoning 'summer love' type relationship through a gentle, eight minute story. What is affirming is how Unilever is targeting 20-somethings with an advertisement which a brand manager, even five years ago, is unlikely to have commissioned. Meanwhile, Facebook, Android and Google regularly run visible campaigns celebrating LGBT equality during Pride month.

These are indeed welcome and positive moves compared with flies in the ointment such as Katy Perry evidently considering it okay to release a single entitled 'Ur so gay' in 2008 and Alan Carr's (PETA, 2014) questionable stance when criticised for urging us all to 'Be a little Fairy for Animals' on behalf of PETA (People for the Ethical Treatment of Animals) and subsequently describing those who were offended by the commercial as 'Oh, so worthy gays.

The most homophobia I get is from gays #selfloathing' (Carr 2014). I find his a surprising reaction since his early act was constructed entirely around the homophobic bullying he suffered as a boy and young man. His celebrity status and fame has allowed him to 'look back and laugh' at these days safe in the knowledge he will never be victimised again as he was before. Evidently this was not the case for Alan Carr back in the day.

Key points

- Gay pupils are often offered few opportunities to acquire coping strategies or learn how to be resilient in the face of homophobic bullying or name-calling.

- Homophobic bullying can affect a pupil's emotional and social wellbeing, not to mention their physical health.

- Coming out takes a great deal of thought and reflection because there is the possibility of losing close friends and being disowned by family.

- A life lived out of authenticity – in which lies are told to others (and even oneself) about who one 'is' – is emotionally exhausting and obstructive to emotional and physical development.

- The hostility demonstrated towards same-sex orientated people by some cultures cannot be underestimated.

CHAPTER 6

How to Respond: Practical Advice

In this chapter three fundamentals are covered. First, how we should respond to verbal and physical homophobic bullying. Second, what reporting mechanisms can and should be put in place to prevent homophobic bullying in the future and third, what sanctions and celebrations of achievement regarding homophobic bullying should look like.

Although we often hear the criminal justice system referring to its adoption of a 'zero-tolerance' approach towards certain crimes, and schools both in the UK and the USA ran with this in the 1990s and throughout the noughties, it should be acknowledged today that adopting a similar approach to homophobic bullying without putting measures in place to help pupils understand *why* it is entirely unacceptable will ultimately fail. Children will not simply 'get over' someone in their class coming out as gay.

Responding to incidents of homophobic bullying should go hand in hand with prevention. Where bullying behaviours are predicated on prejudiced views it is vital that your school engages critically with these attitudes and takes action to deal with both the behaviour and the attitudes underpinning it. Further guidance on preventing homophobic bullying can be found in Chapter 9.

Your school must make it clear to your pupils that homophobic comments are as serious as racist comments and homophobic bullying as serious as other forms. Your school should respond consistently and effectively to incidents of homophobic bullying. This will indicate that they are taken seriously and encourage their reporting whilst discouraging those perpetrating them.

It will already have procedures in place to respond to incidents of bullying and these procedures, where appropriate, should be applied to incidents of homophobic bullying. Procedures need to:

- de-escalate and stop the persistence of homophobic bullying

- protect the pupil(s) experiencing homophobic bullying

- hold to account the pupil(s) perpetrating it in a reasonable, proportionate and consistent way

- apply relevant sanctions to the pupil(s) involved and ensure they learn from the incident

- restore, as far as possible, good relationships between pupils.

Part of these procedures will include helping pupils understand why homophobic bullying is unacceptable. This will mean having age-appropriate dialogue with year or tutor groups about lesbian, gay and bisexual people, their rights in society and laws affecting the pupils once they enter the world of work and wider society in general.

Responding to verbal incidents

Staff should feel able to discuss issues of homophobic bullying with pupils and parents and deal with incidents quickly and effectively before situations escalate. Phrases such as 'That's so gay!' and homophobic language are often used without consideration and it is too frequently ignored because teachers have not been taught how and why they should respond and too many lack confidence to challenge homophobia if they recognise it. Homophobic language in schools has to be challenged because, not only is it a micro-aggression in and of itself, ignoring it propogates a culture of homophobia and bullying will surely follow.

Homophobic language should be challenged within a general programme of work the school undertakes in challenging the problem of homophobic bullying and negative attitudes towards gay people. This is not a singular response to the difficulties that arise. Any action to challenge homophobic language should be taken within the framework of the school's behaviour policy. Staff cannot and will not intervene effectively and consistently if it is not part of the school's policies and procedures.

Casual homophobic language is common in schools but if it is not challenged pupils will think that homophobia is acceptable and they will leave school remaining steadfast to this view. This is when they will come unstuck: either in the workplace or the street where homophobia will not be tolerated by co-workers or members of society going about their everyday lives. The police will recognise reported incidents as 'hate crime': an offence punishable by law. It is therefore important to challenge homophobic language whenever it occurs in our schools.

If you hear a pupil use homophobic language you should intervene appropriately explaining that it is unacceptable, offensive and a form of discrimination. Boxes 6.1 and 6.2 provide practical guidance on how to intervene whether you are in a primary or secondary school. It may seem time consuming at first to challenge a pupil every time you hear the phrase 'That's so gay!' Eventually however pupils will tire of being challenged. If coupled with effective prevention initiatives pupils will not only recognise that they are not allowed to use this language in school but begin to understand why it is unacceptable and even challenge the language themselves.

Of course some pupils will take more time to understand the importance of this issue. They will need to understand the sanctions that will apply if they continue to use this language. If it remains a repeat issue you may want to consider the school's hierarchy of sanctions. Further information about working with those who bully is available in Chapter 7.

Box 6.1 Responding to verbal incidents in primary school

Primary school pupils may not understand that their comments are inappropriate. When you hear a pupil use homophobic language you should consider the following points when dealing with the situation:

- Do they understand the word that has been used and its meaning?

- Do they understand the difference between heterosexual people and gay people?

- Are there any motivating factors concerning the pupil's behaviour? For example are they targeting someone who has lesbian or gay parents or does not behave like a 'typical' boy or girl?

- Do they realise that the comment was inappropriate and hurtful?

- Do they understand the difference between appropriate use of the word gay, for example, and inappropriate uses?

- Have they apologised for their behaviour and to the individual they were targeting?

Box 6.2 Responding to verbal incidents in secondary school

Pupils in secondary school are more likely to have an awareness of lesbian and gay people and for their comments to be based on actual prejudice or ignorance. If you hear a secondary school pupil use homophobic language you should consider the following when dealing with the situation:

- Does the pupil(s) understand that they have been homophobic?

- Are they targeting someone who is lesbian or gay or perceived to be? Do they understand that they are treating the pupil differently because they think or know that they are gay?

- If the pupils are targeting someone who is perceived to be gay do not confirm nor deny these 'accusations'. The actual sexual orientation of the target is irrelevant to the issue, which is that they are being homophobic. Affirm the target's right to come to an understanding of their sexual orientation on their own terms.

- Has the pupil considered the effect that their language and behaviour is having on the target?

- Does the pupil acknowledge that what they are doing is bullying and understand it in the context of prejudice?

- Does the pupil recognise the hierarchy of sanctions which apply for engaging in homophobic bullying?

- Has the pupil considered how they might change their behaviour in the future?

Responding to physical incidents

Pupils may be reluctant to report any bullying incident because they fear that staff will assume they are gay, possibly disapprove and be in a race to tell their parents. Physical bullying immediately indicates a young person is at risk and the school's overarching strategies implemented to safeguard pupils could very well be required here, involving the school's child protection officer, agencies such as EACH and possibly the police if the physical harm quite clearly constitutes a crime. Homophobic violence can quite easily be a crime and schools' anti-bullying policies should be rigorously enforced and regularly updated to keep pupils safe from physical abuse.

Physical abuse can include hitting, punching or kicking (see Table 1.1 in Chapter 1 for a comprehensive illustration). Young people also report that they experience being threatened with a weapon even receive death threats.

Homophobic physical abuse can also include sexual abuse. Some young gay women report that they have experienced sexual abuse and humiliation from both heterosexual girls and boys. Other young people who are lesbian or gay feel under pressure to have sex with someone of the same sex to 'prove' that they 'really are gay'. Some also feel pressured into having sex with someone of the opposite sex to 'prove' they are not gay. These pressures can be heightened by physical abuse and pressure from peers. Physical abuse is a definite indication that staff will need to take steps to safeguard a pupil. Further guidance about dealing with disclosures is available in Chapter 8.

Physical homophobic bullying can affect anyone, regardless of whether or not they are gay, and has to be challenged and stopped within a school.

Primary school pupils can experience both verbal and physical homophobic bullying motivated by the fact that a child seems 'different' from their peers and teachers should recognise this and intervene. Challenging homophobic bullying must start in our primary and elementary schools if we are to end it in our high schools.

All staff members should regularly refresh their awareness of their school's anti-bullying policy and its 'hierarchy of sanctions' when responding to homophobic bullying. When intervening in a physical incident it may be possible to follow the same lines of enquiry as employed when intervening in verbal incidents. Any incident of physical bullying however will need to be coupled with an appropriate sanction even if it is an isolated incident. If the issue is ongoing in necessary circumstances the school will need to consider permanent exclusion (see Box 6.3).

Box 6.3 Guidance for exclusions

The Department for Education's guidance on exclusions (2012) states:

A decision to exclude a pupil should be taken only:

a. In response to serious breaches of the school's behaviour policy; and

b. If allowing the pupil to remain in school would seriously harm the education or welfare of the pupil or others in the school.

Only the Headteacher in charge of a Pupil Referral Unit (or, in the absence of the Head or teacher in charge, the most senior teacher who is acting in that role) can exclude a pupil.

In cases where a head has permanently excluded a pupil for: persistent and defiant misbehaviour, including bullying (which would include racist or homophobic bullying), or repeated possession and/or use of an illegal drug on school premises, the Secretary of State would not normally expect the governing body or an Independent Appeal Panel to reinstate the pupil.

Dealing with homophobic bullying consistently

All staff should be consistent in indicating that homophobic comments are unacceptable and ensure that pupils who experience it feel supported. Staff need to be sensitive when talking to pupils about incidents, taking into account the concerns or worries the pupil may have, and this is addressed in Chapter 8.

If a pupil uses homophobic language all members of staff must point out the effect their language is having on other people remembering that phrases such as 'That's so gay' are not harmless banter but part of homophobia whether the pupil appreciates this or not. All of your staff must be signed up to this too.

Monitoring and recording homophobic bullying incidents

Most schools have mechanisms for recording incidents of bullying. Monitoring incidents enables a school to identify patterns of behaviour, the behaviour's extent and then take proactive steps to challenge it. It is best practice that schools record all incidents of bullying (and acknowledge its different forms) including homophobic bullying. Schools that use monitoring processes are able to modify their bullying policies to respond to specific trends and issues. Incorporating incidents of homophobic bullying into these existing systems, and sharing this information among staff is an invaluable means of raising awareness about the issue amongst everyone.

It is important that recording procedures are detailed and comprehensive enough to allow for effective analysis. If information about what should be recorded and how is not clearly outlined to staff the quality and detail of recording can vary enormously. Without sufficient and detailed data bullying incidents cannot be robustly scrutinised and patterns may be missed. In addition to recording the particulars of incidents, monitoring procedures should also keep a record of the action taken, by whom and when, along with an indication of any follow-ups undertaken to ensure the intervention was effective. With regard to homophobic bullying it is all too common for pupils to report that school interventions were ineffective and even exacerbated the problem. By recording the actions taken in response to reported and recorded incidents schools are in a stronger position to investigate whether these interventions were successful and change their approach if necessary.

An effective anti-bullying log should include:

- a clear definition of bullying including prejudice-based bullying so staff are clear on what they need to record

- a detailed account of the incident including where and when it took place, who was involved including target, perpetrator and any bystanders, the nature of the incident and whether it was prejudice based (homophobic, sexist, racist, disablist, etc.)

- actions to be taken, by whom and by when.

In common with other forms of bullying not all incidents of homophobic bullying will be reported to teachers and staff. Pupils may lack confidence in bullying interventions and fear the repercussions of admitting they are a target of homophobia. In 2014 North Somerset Council included specific questions about homophobic bullying in its authority-wide survey completed by its schools. Therefore be sure to include questions about homophobic bullying on anonymous pupil surveys in your own school or authority. Sexual orientation (real or perceived) was the second most common motivator for bullying (the first was weight). This insight prompted local schools to implement lessons and tutorial time that addressed the issue of homophobic bullying.

Evaluating progress also makes it easy to celebrate success and helps those involved keep focussed and motivated. Schools should evaluate progress every term, reporting back to all stakeholders, especially pupils. This will help show progress as well as what is remaining to be done.

Sanctions

A school should establish how its range of sanctions can be applied most appropriately to the varying severity of homophobic bullying.

A mapping exercise can be used as a professional development and discussion tool with all staff and governors to develop a shared understanding and consistency of practice in applying sanctions to those who perpetrate homophobic bullying. Participants are given a series of, preferably actual, scenarios of homophobic bullying, or wider descriptive statements, and then asked to map them against the school sanctions framework (see Box 6.4).

Box 6.4 Homophobic bullying scenarios

Jenny, age 13
Jenny has been experiencing homophobic bullying for several months. A group of girls in her year have spread rumours about her sexual orientation, exclude her from activities and call her 'the lezzer'. Jenny has reported the incident to her tutor and asked for help.

Ahmed, age 15
Ahmed reports that there is homophobic graffiti written about him in the toilet and that he knows who wrote it.

Rachel, Amy and Jess, age 16
Amy and Jess have recently started a romantic relationship. Although Amy has been out as a lesbian for a year Jess has only recently told her friends that she is bisexual. Rachel feels left out when the two girls spend all their time together and don't invite her. She starts spreading rumours that Jess is sleeping around and the relationship with Amy is just an experiment. This upsets both Amy and Jess and they stop talking to Rachel, leaving her isolated from her friends.

Joe, age 14
Joe has recently come out on Facebook as gay. He thought that if he told people in person they were more likely to spread rumours whereas on Facebook people might not notice. Unfortunately many of his Facebook friends did notice and wrote homophobic and nasty comments on his Facebook wall. Joe told his mum who reported it to the school.

Ryan and Lee, age 6
Ryan and Lee are in the playground playing tag. When Lee trips over and begins crying you overhear Ryan call him a 'gay boy'.

Evie, age 7
Evie spends her lunch break playing football with the boys. When she returns from lunch her friends laugh at her and say she can't sit on the girls' table because she is a boy.

Responding to incidents of homophobic bullying should be undertaken with acknowledging the 'hierarchy of sanctions' which a school has deemed appropriate for responding to inappropriate behaviour. This helps staff respond effectively to bullying. The sanctions should be developed in consultation with pupils and their views. When determining sanctions it is helpful to consider the following questions adapted from the Welsh Government's (2011) guidance on homophobic bullying:

- What sanctions should apply if a pupil uses homophobic language such as 'That's so gay!' unintentionally and it is not directed towards anyone?

- How can sanctions be used when homophobic language is directed at an individual or group, for example, 'You're so gay!'?

- How will sanctions escalate if the bullying behaviour is continual?

- Should sanctions be different if the pupil targeted by homophobic bullying is not gay?

- How should sanctions be used if a pupil is targeted because their friend, parent or other family member is gay?

- What strategies can you employ to deal with a group who are bullying an individual?

- If a pupil is gay or bisexual but does not want their parents to know, how will you keep parents informed of the bullying they are experiencing?

- Could EACH or another training provider assist the school, the target(s), the perpetrator(s) or their families?

Sanctions should also be visible and well publicised within school to pupils, parents, staff and governors. It is important that all stakeholders are aware of the consequences of homophobic bullying, their rights and responsibilities and the sanctions they may experience should they engage in this prejudice-based bullying.

Celebrating success

Whilst no one wants to have to apply sanctions (because it indicates unacceptable behaviour has been exacted) we know there are times when this must be implemented. What so many schools forget to do is celebrate achievements and success in challenging bullying (including homophobic bullying). Celebration elevates achievements around anti-bullying work to be shared by the whole school and fosters a culture of positiveness and an affirmative school ethos. Celebrating success helps to assure pupils, staff, governors and parents that the school is taking meaningful, effective steps to improve policy and practice.

Here are some of the ways in which your school can celebrate successes concerning homophobic bullying:

- Demonstrate in assemblies the role of mentors or nominated members of staff (in secondary schools) or playground buddies (in primary/elementary schools) in challenging homophobic bullying. Explain why it is vital never to be a bystander or to collude in others' bullying.

- Use the outcomes of a review by pupils and staff of your school's anti-bullying policy as a way to engage the whole school in recognising what is already being done and what still must be done.

- Use the Ofsted Self Evaluation Form to identify and report outcomes of your school's anti-bullying work.

- Use a range of national and locally validated schemes to celebrate achievements in challenging bullying such as the Bullying Intervention Group Award or Diana Award for anti-bullying work.

- Schools in a partnership or federation may opt to run a joint conference on, for example, human rights or equalities issues and focus on prejudice-based bullying or harassment.

This could examine school, local, national and international issues. Remember to invite local agencies to input into this such as your local council's Equalities Team Lead.

Key points

- Responding to incidents should go hand in hand with prevention.

- All staff should be consistent in indicating that homophobic bullying is unacceptable and ensure that pupils who experience it feel supported.

- Responding to incidents of homophobic bullying should recognize the 'hierarchy of sanctions' which a school has deemed appropriate for responding to inappropriate behaviour.

- Monitoring incidents enables you to identify patterns of behaviour and the extent of the bullying and to take proactive steps to challenge it.

- Celebrating successful anti-bullying work elevates its achievements and fosters a positive culture.

CHAPTER 7

Working with Those Who Bully

We know that bullying is unwanted, aggressive behaviour which involves a real or perceived power imbalance. The behaviour is repeated, or has the potential to be, over time. Both children who are bullied and those who bully can experience lasting mental health issues.

Working with those who bully homophobically is challenging as it is often perpetrated by the most powerful pupils who command other pupils' attention, and even that of their teachers, either by being 'popular' with pupils, teachers or both or through being 'a force to be reckoned with'. These pupils are not, in truth, lastingly 'popular' but they are potent and influential. We know that in bullying there is an imbalance of power, sometimes achieved through physical strength and sometimes attained by manipulation (using access to information to humiliate, harm or control others). Bear in mind that power imbalances can change over time and in different situations even if the same people are involved.

I often witness cases where pupils consider their bullying behaviour justified and regularly witness how parents attempt to justify their child's bullying if either the child or the parents are challenged. It is not uncommon for pupils who bully to experience a home life where there is scant positive, caring adult attention, where discipline is inconsistent and 'binary' (proffering too much privilege countered with punitive sanctions for misdemeanours) with some parents being either emotionally or physically aggressive, or both. It is hard for such children to develop empathy or sympathy and they regularly fail to make cause and effect links between their actions and consequences. Rather than reflect on their behaviour when punished for bullying others they will resent adults in authority or their peers whom they have bullied. Where sanctions for bullying are largely absent or inconsistent young people who enjoy the power and social status gained from it are very unlikely to change. Without supervision, clear expectations and consistent consequences this is practically a given.

When responding to an incident of homophobic bullying you should consider how your response can alter the behaviour and attitudes of the perpetrator along with any bystanders who may support or reinforce the perpetrator's actions. As outlined in Chapter 4, homophobic bullying is underpinned by a range of attitudes, values and beliefs. It is important we understand the perpetrator's motivations for targeting someone homophobically before deciding on the action to take. You and others who work with young people in a professional capacity play a vital role in changing the behaviour of those who bully. For interventions and responses to be effective you need a clear understanding of the roots of bullying behaviour and a confidence in your school's strategies. It is equally important to realise what approaches can inadvertently make the bullying worse.

When considering the root of the bullying behaviour the following questions can help:

- Does your pupil understand that homophobic bullying is not acceptable in their school?

- Do they understand why?

- Does your pupil understand the impact their actions have had on the pupil experiencing the homophobic bullying? Do they recognise what they have done?

- Does your pupil think their actions are justified?

- Does your pupil understand that homophobic language is unacceptable however inadvertently used: 'Oh God, that is SO gay!'?

Pupils cannot be expected to learn by themselves that homophobic bullying is unacceptable. If they do not know why they need to be told. Pupils who have not been taught previously that homophobic bullying is wrong will take time to realise their behaviour is inappropriate. In the short term any incident of bullying needs to be dealt with by employing the appropriate sanctions as agreed in your school policy. This might not have occurred to you before but a bully not prevented from bullying or made to see the absolute inappropriateness of their actions will rarely stop bullying. Continuation of bullying will:

- prompt a group culture where causing harm by bullying is seen as acceptable and everyone tacitly accepts collusion with bullying as the norm

- demonstrate that the school either condones the behaviour and attitudes which underlie it, seems powerless to prevent it (being thwarted by even greater issues) or does not care

- in most cases, lead a young person to become an adult who causes harm to others by engaging in anti-social, harassing and potentially criminal behaviour.

Any time an incident of homophobic bullying occurs your school must respond and demonstrate that this behaviour is not condoned. A strategic approach to sanctions and interventions is explored in Chapter 6. Your school anti-bullying policy and staff training should clearly cover the agreed procedure for responding to a bullying incident including the sanctions, reporting procedures and whether the pupil's parents should be informed. The pupil must acknowledge the harm they have caused and why the actions are in breach of school policy. To encourage pupils to think about the consequences of their actions consider these points:

- Does your pupil recognise that action needs to be taken to make the bullied pupil feel better? Does your pupil accept responsibility? It is crucial they understand they must take responsibility for making the situation better. They should be urged to generate suggestions concerning next steps and recognise that the bullied person will have their own views.

- Will your pupil make assurances that they will not bully someone again? Do they understand that the incident cannot be repeated? The pupil must understand that the key to resolving the incident is a commitment not to reoffend. They must appreciate the importance of a general change in their behaviour.

- Does your pupil understand what other sanctions will apply if they continue to bully? Are they clear about the escalation process and how this can ultimately end in exclusion? Pupils should not be discouraged from expressing their views about gay people and issues but they need to understand the difference between expressing an opinion and being insulting.

Ignorance

Building on points made above, if pupils do not fully understand why homophobic bullying is wrong when sanctioned or punished, instead of reflecting on their own behaviour they are likely to blame authority figures or peers whom they have distressed. This can lead to ramifications or the problem escalating for the target.

Responding to one-off incidents of homophobic bullying can only go so far and to truly eradicate the problem a longer-term strategy needs to be implemented. Pupils who bully often have a negative view of school and its role. School culture cannot be underestimated for its role in fostering bullying. Make use of curriculum opportunities, work in partnership with pupils, parents and governors to develop policies and ensure everyone knows in advance and accepts sanctions which will be applied if pupils fail to follow the rules. Ultimately, only dialogue and discussion about sexual orientation held in a positive, constructive arena will change your school's culture. This will not happen if the topic is only ever discussed in direct connection with homophobic bullying. Further guidance on how to implement this long-term strategy is detailed in Chapters 9 and 10.

Behavioural problems

For some pupils, bullying and other forms of social aggression are more related to impulsiveness and poor social skills than to an effort to control others. When this is true, cognitive-behavioural interventions to improve impulse control and structured social skills training may also be helpful. Anger management strategies may be effective with these pupils although these are unlikely to help a pupil whose aggression is planned and executed with pre-meditation.

Bullying can also be a response to emotional distress or mental health issues. Too often this is overlooked and little attention is paid to the emotional wellbeing and mental health of those who bully. In 2014 the UK Government issued specific guidance on *Mental Health and Behaviour in Schools* to help teachers better identify underlying mental health problems within pupils and prevent them from being wrongly labelled as troublemakers (DfE, 2014a). Promoting positive mental health should go hand in hand with work around behaviour and bullying.

There are a number of approaches which may be considered to stop a bully bullying. One might believe that they have low self-esteem and need work to build this up. Aggressive pupils can, in actual fact, have very high self-esteem, their aggression emanating from a sense of privilege and entitlement (invariably imbued in them by their parents). It is rarely effective to employ counselling strategies based on building self-esteem with an aggressive child.

You might wish to consider peer mediation. Mediation-based strategies are based frequently on the assumption that both parties have done something wrong. When carried out by young or relatively untrained mediators, however, mediation in bullying situations risks solidifying the power differential between the young person who bullies and the bullied young person.

Effective interventions with a pupil who bullies often involve strategies such as reality therapy or cognitive-behaviour therapies which make them accountable for their actions and for the impact of those actions on themselves and others. Work with family systems and consultation and advocacy with schools are also often necessary. As William Glasser (1975) wrote in *Reality Therapy*, '[In therapy] someone cares enough about the patient to make him face a truth he has spent his life trying to avoid: he is responsible for his own behaviour.' (p.27)

Effective interventions are built on the following principles adapted from the US Department of Health and Human Services guidance (2011):

- Have in place a contingency for unexpected outcomes along a continuum starting from non-hostile but ongoing to escalating and increasingly damaging consequences. The aim is to make the perpetrator recognise the cost of their bullying behaviour and guide them to consider alternative behaviour.

- Hold the pupil who bullies to account for their actions. Confront excuses that minimise the behaviour ('It was just a bit of banter') or externalise the cause of the behaviour ('He was acting gay so I hit him'). Ensure the pupil fully acknowledges their behaviour. Emphasise that they had other options and that no matter what the provocation, only they are fully responsible for their decision to bully.

- Support parents and colleagues in holding their children or pupils to account for their actions and not to allow rationalisations ('She only gets into mischief because she's so bright and isn't challenged enough academically').

- Once your pupil is able to recognise significant problems with their behaviour, mental health professionals can work with them in establishing goals for improvement. The pupil's progress can be monitored and tracked. The pupil can have this reflected back at them as they demonstrate improvements and develop a sense of pride in what they are achieving. If we work with the pupil on specifics such as asking them to identify precisely what they hoped to achieve by a particular bullying behaviour we can work towards finding other ways to gain a sense of reward that is not connected to subjugating someone else to make the child doing the bullying feel better about themselves. A lot of this revolves around dealing with anger management issues in the child. If you can get to the root of why they are angry you are already half way to making their bullying stop.

- Assist the pupil in building better relations with their family members and school mentors.

- Support parents and siblings to both acknowledge and endorse improved behaviour in their family member, affirming non-aggressive ways of behaving with child-relevant rewards.

- Nurture genuinely felt emotions such as empathy and sympathy to help your pupil understand and recognise the ramifications of their behaviour. It is important however that we do not maintain this 'learning' at purely a cognitive level. If we do this there is the chance that we help our pupil to get even better at bullying; once they understand how and what hurts people they can get even better at doing it!

- Develop your pupil's sense of 'conscience'. Once they recognise how their bullying behaviour has caused them to be sanctioned or punished they can begin to appreciate the effect of their actions upon their targets.

Pupils who believe their actions are justified

Some pupils will believe that their homophobic behaviour is justified and this can often be reinforced by parents. Even if pupils and parents have certain religious or moral views about gay people this does not mean that bullying people should be in any way tolerated. It will be helpful to consider the questions below when dealing with a pupil who feels that their homophobic behaviour is justified:

- Are you and your school colleagues confident to raise or respond to issues of sexual orientation even when your pupils express challenging or disconcerting opinions? Do all your pupils recognise the difference between a committed viewpoint, intransigence and bigotry?

- Have your school's pupils and parents had it explained explicitly that homophobic bullying will not be tolerated and why and how their personal view of gay people can be at odds with the school's stance on challenging homophobic bullying? Does everyone connected to the school understand the difference?

- Are both pupils and parents aware of your school's policies relevant to homophobic bullying? Do they understand that any negative behaviour manifested by their child could well have serious ramifications?

- Do your pupils and parents appreciate that sanctions are in place with regard to homophobic bullying and these plus accordant punishments will be applied equally regarding homophobic bullying?

Pupils should not be discouraged from expressing their views about gay people and related issues but they should be taught the difference between expressing an opinion and self-consciously being derogatory. Both pupils and parents must understand that their personal views (including religious ones) can never justify bullying.

Parents need to appreciate the severity of homophobic bullying and understand what sanctions will apply if they are to help prevent bullying. They should be made aware that, in the UK, schools have a legal duty to respond to and prevent homophobic bullying in accordance with the Equality Act 2010, Public Sector Equality Duty 2011 and Education and Inspections Act 2006.

If parents are considered a significant factor in the child's behaviour and are unwilling to engage voluntarily with either the local authority or the school itself it may be appropriate to consider a parenting order. A parenting order is a civil court order which consists of two elements:

- a requirement on the parent to attend counselling or guidance sessions (e.g. parenting education or parenting support classes) where they will receive help and support to enable them to improve their child's behaviour or attendance – this is the core of the parenting order and lasts for three months

- a requirement on the parent to comply with such requirements as are determined necessary by the court for improving their child's behaviour or attendance at school. This element can last up to 12 months.

Homophobic language

Many schools will be indicating consistently that homophobic bullying is wrong and pupils will recognise that it is unacceptable to treat someone differently because they are gay or are thought to be. Where schools often struggle is with the use of homophobic language and phrases such as 'That's so gay'. In these cases pupils will often not see that their actions have a direct consequence for anyone. As a result it will often be perceived as 'harmless banter'. When so much legislative progress has been made for lesbian, gay and bisexual equality, pupils might question whether co-opting the word 'gay' as an insult really matters. Language changes all the time and many young people will argue that calling their homework gay has nothing to do with their opinions on same-sex relationships. In fact often young people who identify as lesbian, gay or bisexual will use 'That's so gay' in this context. For these pupils the word can have several meanings which they think has no connection to their attitudes towards themselves and other gay people. There is also a chance pro-behaviour is at play here. This is when someone who is conscious of feeling 'outside' of society's 'mainstream' deploys usually self-deprecating humour to divert attention away from their, for example, disability, ethnicity or sexuality. It sometimes works but to those who can see what is happening it is more often embarrassing.

The structured prompts adapted from East Sussex and Brighton Hove PSHE Advisory Team are useful practical tips for dealing with homophobic language (2002) (see Box 7.1). They provide staff with a variety of simple responses, each operating at a varying degree of remove from the situation.

Box 7.1 Structured prompts for homophobic language

1. Dismissive response:

    'I'm not prepared to listen to language like that.'

    'I really don't want to have to hear remarks such as this.'

2. Interrogative response:

    'What makes you say that?'

    'What did you mean by that?'

    'Shall we talk about why people think like this?'

3. Didactic response:

    'Language like that is unacceptable.'

    'We have a rule in school about the use of homophobic language.'

4. Personal response:

    'I'm not happy with what you've said.'

    'I find that language really offensive.'

    'What you've said really disturbs me.'

5. Organisational response:

    'Our school doesn't tolerate language like that.'

    'A lot of people would find that remark really offensive.'

However, to punish pupils for this use of language without discussion can propagate its use and fail to engage with the real experiences of young people (Monk, 2011). To assume homophobic attitudes without listening to young people's views is to pre-judge and censor them. The problem here is that beyond the banal banter of calling homework 'gay' these young people have few opportunities to express their attitudes constructively around sexuality. We must never allow young people to brush us or their peers off with 'But I never meant nothing by it' but staff dealing with the inappropriate use of homophobic language need to feel confident when responding to it. Allowing it to go unchallenged will only appear to reinforce its acceptability in our classrooms, corridors and playgrounds. Challenging homophobic name-calling and bullying should be combined with opportunities to explore and reflect upon pupils' experiences, values and knowledge to ensure they understand the impact of their actions. Staff need to feel safe and confident in addressing homophobia and in most schools professional input is going to be required from a nationally recognised and qualified agency such as EACH.

Engaging the local community

Schools will be aware of the range of views and attitudes regarding issues of gender and sexual orientation and many will be educating pupils who come from backgrounds where there exist divergent and conflicting views on both. Some individuals or sections of society may question or reject the principles of gender and sexual orientation equality but every school is required by law to uphold these principles. Discussing bullying is a great place to begin engaging your pupils with these sensitive issues and your school will need to make use of a full range of strategies when working to engage with parents, families and communities including:

- clearly communicating your school's position on all forms of bullying and being explicit in naming homophobic bullying in all your relevant policies

- using every means available to keep your parents informed about your school's stance on issues of bullying: your school prospectus, newsletters, website, social media platforms, homework diaries and myriad communications available to your school office

- ensuring your parents know how they can report and seek help concerning homophobic bullying

- offering tailored support to parents who need this either because their child is experiencing bullying or due to their child's bullying behaviour

- utilise the formal mechanisms already in place for parental engagement including the use of parenting contracts or home-school agreements. A lot of parents are only too pleased to receive your school's help.

If you do not feel that any of the above are currently robust enough in your school raise this with your manager or the senior leadership team as appropriate.

A strategic approach to applying sanctions and interventions

Your school needs to establish how the range of sanctions available to it can be applied most appropriately to different incidences of homophobic bullying. As mentioned in Chapter 6, a mapping exercise can be used as a professional development and discussion tool with all staff and governors to develop a shared understanding and consistency of practice in applying sanctions to those who participate in homophobic bullying. Participants are given a series of, preferably actual, scenarios of homophobic bullying or wider descriptive statements and are then asked to map them against the school sanctions framework.

Implementing permanent exclusions and involving the police

Homophobic behaviour in your school may involve criminal offences, such as assault, theft, criminal damage, harassment, misuse of communications, prejudice-based crime (hate crime) or sexual offences. Where bullying is particularly serious or persistent it will be necessary (either to protect the person experiencing the bullying or respond appropriately to an incident) to implement exclusions (temporary or permanent) or involve the police in dealing with criminal offences that have been committed (see Box 7.2). Your school's senior management team will need to follow the procedures they have put in place for involving the police in cases of this nature.

Key points

- Pupils will rarely if ever change their homophobic bullying behaviour if they are not brought to an understanding of why – from inadvertent use of 'That's so gay' to violence – it is never acceptable.

- Pupils with additional needs will need a bespoke approach to help them understand why homophobic name-calling and bullying is wrong.

- Where incidents can be managed in school this is always the best policy. Involving the police should only be a last resort but in certain circumstances will be unavoidable.

- Consult everyone concerning your approach to challenging homophobic bullying. You will achieve far greater buy-in from parents if the governors or trustees and teachers have devised your school's approach with your parents and pupils and then published it on your website.

- Whilst making it crystal clear what is the school's tier of sanctions be sure to celebrate milestones reflecting achievements and strides the whole school has made in reducing all incidents of bullying including homophobic.

CHAPTER 8

Sensitive Handling of Disclosures

The expectation that teachers will respond empathetically or at least sympathetically to a pupil disclosing that they have been a target of bullying is a given but when that bullying is homophobic in nature it is particularly important to be sensitive to their situation and needs. Remember, bullying is bullying regardless of a member of staff's religious, cultural or personal convictions, every pupil has a right to be protected from it and you have a duty of care towards each child in your charge.

In fact, pupils may be reluctant to speak to members of staff precisely because they feel sensitive issues will have to be shared widely and all school staff should be aware of how to handle pupil disclosures of a personal nature. Most gay pupils who do not experience homophobic bullying are unlikely to find the need to come out to a teacher. It may be known that some pupils are gay across the school if, for example, they are in a visible relationship with another pupil. Most gay pupils will only be out to their friends or a close knit network.

Learning a pupil is gay either because they or their friends tell you is not necessarily a disclosure. It is often just a simple statement of fact about their lives. It is important in these moments to still offer affirmation and support but not undue concern. After all, pupils being comfortably out and gay in your school is a positive sign and testament to your school's inclusive ethos. If you were to learn that a heterosexual pupil fancied a classmate it would not see you reaching for the crisis pamphlets or calling home unless you had reasonable cause for concern. The same judgement should be applied when supporting gay or lesbian pupils.

Even if there is a visible lesbian and gay student body within your school, an LGBT forum in the UK or a Gay, Straight Alliance (GSA) in your USA school, there will more likely than not be pupils who are not out or are unsure of their sexual orientation. Partially down to the lack of existence of 'out' positive role models within a school, pupils can still fear homophobic discrimination particularly if they do not have access to a supportive network of family and friends. These pupils may be more likely to become the target of rumour-mongering, gossip and more. Interestingly, pupils in schools EACH supports note that those who are 'suspected' of being gay are far more likely to be bullied than those who are openly gay. Regardless of sexual orientation, all pupils can perpetrate this kind of bullying behaviour particularly if they do not yet possess the emotional maturity to understand that not everyone finds it easy to come to terms with their sexual orientation. One should challenge any speculation about another pupil's sexual orientation highlighting that this too is unhelpful and affirming all pupils' right to come to an understanding of their identity on their own terms.

Too often homophobic bullying can result in pupils being 'outed' before they are ready. When you are the teacher faced with responding to a pupil's disclosure of homophobic bullying you may as likely as not be dealing with their coming out simultaneously. Of course not all pupils who are homophobically bullied are gay and not all gay pupils are homophobically bullied. Yet even those heterosexual pupils who are targeted may find themselves questioning their sexual orientation as a result of the homophobic bullying. It is important that all permutations are dealt with sensitively and on the pupil's own terms.

Your school's confidentiality policy should provide a framework for staff when deciding whether or not they can offer confidentiality to a pupil who discloses information about themselves or their situation and this is explored in more detail below.

The reality is that a member of staff – whatever their role in the school – can offer only a degree of confidentiality. Where a member of staff is concerned that the pupil may be at risk of harm they must make contact with the school's safeguarding lead in order to discuss making a referral according to its procedures.

Staff should also be clear on distinguishing their own needs from those of the pupil. For example, if a young person discloses themselves as gay, the member of staff may need to look up further information or guidance on the issue in general as a response to a request from the young person. So long as no child protection issues present themselves during the course of your conversation your duty of care to the pupil is to preserve their confidentiality.

Health service staff operating a service on your school site (e.g. a school nurse) offer a slightly different degree of confidentiality although the principle of a confidentiality that is limited according to whether or not the pupil is at risk is consistent. Health service staff are bound by the same limited confidentiality within the class environment as teachers and other school staff.

As much as the internet offers pupils a window onto the world around them it does not educate them in the same way that a trusted adult can. The internet offers possibilities but it is not always safe and students need the support of adults to guide them through the usual storm and stress of young adulthood. Any gay pupil who needs our support but who goes without it will not thrive. At best they will switch off, coast through school and academically under-achieve. Too many however run the grave risk of becoming depressed (even if they do not recognise they are) or turn to some form of self-harming behaviour (smoking, drinking, drug-taking or eating disorders) which occasionally does not manifest itself until adulthood.

A rite of passage enjoyed by the majority of heterosexual teenagers can so often be unavailable to the average gay teenager, particularly those in rural areas or in families where adherence to strict opposite sex cultural activity is profound. Outlets for sexual curiosity can then become internet chat rooms, pornography or geosocial websites. In all such places people may not be who they seem and a young person's subsequent introduction to such people and sexual relationships can be dangerous, with fewer of the inherent safeguards and social pleasures enjoyed by their heterosexual peers.

So, the next time you find yourself experiencing a 'doorknob moment' (someone telling you something really important and about which you should do something just as they have their hand on the doorknob and are poised to leave) it is not beyond the realms of possibility that one of your pupils is about to tell you that they are gay or that they are experiencing homophobic bullying or both. I say 'you' because you have picked up this book and you are interested in what it has to say. Colleagues in your school whom you would not seek out if you needed a friendly ear and reassuring words will not be sought out by your pupils either, and, in all likelihood, unless they have been directed to by their manager, will not read this book.

How can you be best prepared for such a disclosure by one of your pupils? Well, of course you will be acutely aware that it will have taken them far longer to pluck up the courage to tell you than the time it takes to actually tell you. In fact, your pupil will have mulled over the issue for a very long time before deciding who to approach to discuss it. If they have chosen you it is because they have decided you are a trustworthy, empathetic person who will not judge them harshly but take what they have to say seriously. Good for you! Let us assume however that a pupil is yet to have done so and you wish to be prepared. The individual circumstances of coming out or homophobic bullying will be specific to each pupil and accordingly require bespoke handling. It is possible nevertheless to adhere to the general principles detailed in Box 8.1.

Box 8.1 Handling disclosures of homophobic bullying

1. Bear in mind you are as likely as not to be told about homophobic bullying just as you are leaving for a another lesson/about to have a really important meeting that has been postponed previously and which you really cannot put off again/bursting to go to the loo or restroom which is not close by.

2. Factoring in point 1, it may be necessary to explain to your pupil that you absolutely want to listen to what they have to say and explain calmly and succinctly why at this moment you cannot. Be aware of your non-verbal communication as the pupil may hear one thing but misconstrue your body language, reading your need to be somewhere else as rejection. Above all thank them for beginning the conversation and tell them you are looking forward to its continuance.

3. Arrange with them a time as close to now when you can meet. In the interim offer them someone who can listen to them right now (only if you know that you can), e.g. your school counsellor, nurse or similar and listen to whether this is what they want.

4. When you meet do so in a calm, safe space in which you know will not be interrupted by telephones or other people. Ask them to tell you what is on their mind.

5. Let the pupil get out their opening sentence(s). Prior to any confidential conversation you may have, outline your child protection responsibilities (see 'Confidentiality', p.114). Your pupil may go on to disclose information that you consider harmful (to themselves or others) and this you are legally obliged to act upon. You need to be clear and transparent about the legislative responsibilities you have with regard to disclosures you consider harmful to the pupil. Inform them of the circumstances in which information may need to be shared, with whom and for what purpose. Overarchingly however ensure your pupil understands that, within the child protection parameters you have outlined, what they say will most definitely be treated confidentially.

6. Listen to the rest of their story in a non-judgemental way.

7. If they are disclosing bullying encourage them to agree to the incident being formally logged through the school's system for recording bullying incidents and explain that this can be anonymised if this is their wish.

8. Ask them what they would like you to do to help them.

9. Explain that they, or you on their behalf, may telephone EACH or another support agency, to talk over homophobic bullying, should this be relevant to the pupil.

10. Thank them for talking to you (do not however say 'confiding in you').

Adapted from Save the Children (2008)

Pupils who have experienced homophobic bullying may require immediate support following an incident but they may well also need ongoing support to feel safe in school. Targets of homophobic bullying could need your support to tell their story fully and discuss how the incident has affected them. Reassure the pupil that ongoing support will be made available to them and that you will take action to prevent the same thing happening again to the best of your abilities. You have been honoured with being the recipient of your pupil's disclosure. Now you must honour this responsibility by helping them.

Sources of help to support you might include a colleague who arranges to meet with the pupil to 'check in' on how they are. You may feel that another member of staff is better placed to provide ongoing support than you and you need to explain to your pupil why this is the case and who this person will be. Are there dedicated pupils in the school (peer supporters or mentors) who could complement this role and whom the pupil would feel safe and comfortable talking to about either homophobic bullying or coming out issues? In some cases, both the target of homophobic bullying and its perpetrator (and respective family members) would benefit from specialist intervention. Consider inviting a training provider such as EACH to come to the school to provide targeted support for the pupil or training for the staff to help them support pupils in such situations in future.

In anticipation of a forthcoming meeting with a pupil who you think or know will be discussing either a disclosure around sexual orientation or telling you about homophobic bullying it is worth bearing in mind these points:

- Lesbian, gay or bisexual issues are obviously not simply or just about sexual attraction and sex. There are deep emotions and wider relationships with friends and family to work through.

- Try to reassure your pupil that if they are gay they should feel no pressure to be 'out' and that they should take things at a pace that feels comfortable for them.

- Encourage your pupil to think carefully about who, if anyone at this stage, they want to know that they are gay and why they do or do not want them to know.

- Ask the young person to consider the reaction of those they will tell and any implications. If they are worried about ramifications encourage them to reflect on how they will deal with situations which may arise.

- If they indicate any sense of shame or disgrace about being gay or being homophobically bullied be positive and reassure them that there is nothing wrong with being lesbian, gay or bisexual. Positive affirmations and a supportive environment for gay pupils can help combat any internalised feelings of homophobia which are so often borne out of negative depictions of gay people and the portrayal of heterosexuality as the only and 'normal' way to be.

- If a pupil discloses that they are questioning or are confused about their sexuality you can reassure them that questioning their sexuality is a normal part of the process of developing and understanding their identity. Explain that in time they may identify as heterosexual, lesbian, gay or bisexual. Explore with them what these labels mean and their understanding of sexual orientation (Save the Children, 2008).

- If the pupil discloses that they are engaging in sexual activity or are considering having sex use your professional discretion to determine:

    - whether the young person is capable of understanding and consenting to the sexual activity in which they are or wish to be involved

    - the nature of the relationship between those involved, particularly if there are age or power imbalances which may come within child protection concerns

    - if the pupil is adequately informed about safe sex and has access to appropriate advice.

Within homophobic bullying this may include the disclosure of sexual bullying including the disclosure of potentially criminal acts such as sexual assault. Schools should therefore work to ensure that all staff are confident in their knowledge of its safeguarding referral processes.

If you are concerned that the young person may be at risk of sexual abuse or exploitation a referral should be made to your dedicated safeguarding or child protection officer or, if relevant, Child Exploitation and Online Protection (CEOP).

Confidentiality

Since 2000, when I began supporting teachers, youth workers and others who educate or support young people with regard to coming out or homophobic bullying, I have observed how unassured people are about where they stand on the issue of confidentiality.

As a basic rule, young people have the same right to privacy as adults. If a young person chooses to confide information about themselves this must remain confidential. You have legal responsibilities to pass on information to appropriate agencies if a young person discloses abuse or if not sharing the information would place a young person at risk of significant harm.

A breach of confidentiality occurs when you share information of some sensitivity a) without legitimate purpose; b) without the permission of the person who provided it and c) without the permission of the person to whom it relates – in each case without a justifiable reason for doing so.

Young people who disclose their sexual orientation or come out to you may not have done so to members of their family or to other staff members as they may deem the personal risk too high or expect discrimination or rejection. It is important to note that disclosure of sexual orientation is not a reason to breach a young person's confidentiality. If they also disclose information that places them at risk of significant harm their sexual orientation must still remain private until consent is obtained from the young person to share this information.

Consent must be informed; the person giving consent needs to understand why information needs to be shared, who will see or hear the information, for what purpose, and the implications of it being shared. Even in cases of disclosure of abuse it is best practice to inform your young person why this information is shared, with whom it is shared, and for what purpose.

You should not seek consent if to do so would place a young person at risk of significant harm, or place an adult at risk of significant harm, or would prejudice the prevention or detection of serious crime.

It is still possible to share information for learning purposes amongst staff or in order to develop policy if the information shared does not enable the young person to be identified.

The key factors in disclosing information are as follows:

- Is there a legitimate purpose for you to share the information?

- Does the information enable a person to be identified?

- Is the information confidential?

- If the information is confidential do you have informed consent to share?

- If consent is refused, or there are good reasons not to seek consent to share confidential information, is there sufficient public interest to share information?

- If the decision is to share are you sharing the right information in the right way?

- Have you properly recorded your decision?

It is very possible that either you or your colleagues will have little or no experience of having an openly lesbian, gay or bisexual pupil in the classroom. It will probably come as no surprise therefore that if your school is one where issues of sexual orientation equality and rights are rarely if ever discussed, and homophobia not actively challenged, very few same-sex attracted young people will disclose their sexual orientation to any member of staff whilst at school. However, once homophobic behaviour is challenged comprehensively and a more respectful culture established, your school will need to address the following:

- Disclosures will increase. Pupils will choose to talk individually to teaching or support staff about the bullying behaviours they experience, or even perpetrate, and more generally about their lives and experiences which may involve coming out to you.

- Existing policies will need reviewing. The senior leadership team will need to revise your school's child protection and anti-bullying policies with staff, pupils and parents to accommodate issues related to coming out and homophobic bullying.

- Recording systems will need reviewing. Your school's system for recording incidents is likely to need a new entry for homophobic bullying.

- Information may need updating. Your school probably will need to revise its list of external support agencies to include EACH plus the range of statutory and voluntary agencies which offer complementary support services and training on issues related to prejudice-based bullying (see Appendix 2).

Parents

Finally it is important to make reference to parents and their reaction when they learn either that their child has been the target of homophobic bullying or that they have come out as gay. Parents are usually the adults in whom children feel most confident confiding but sometimes they feel they cannot because they are going to be rejected; this can have devastating results.

Most parents enter into a form of grieving process when they learn or discover their child is gay. Some parents (particularly mothers) recognise their child is gay long before the child realises the fact themselves but many more are shocked, bewildered, angry and only finally accepting of their child's sexuality (this being dependent on a number of factors including individual personalities, religious convictions and culture). Some never accept and become estranged from their child. Some children choose to effect this estrangement themselves because of the degree of negativity shown by the parent. Some have no choice in the matter and are made homeless. In the UK, The Albert Kennedy Trust exists to support young people in this situation whilst in the USA there is the Family Acceptance Project.

Key points

- Reporting homophobic bullying is not the same as coming out as gay however a pupil's disclosure of homophobic bullying may be accompanied by their coming out.

- Gay pupils may be reluctant to report homophobic bullying because they feel they may be 'outed' to their parents or the school before they are ready.

- If a pupil confides private information about themselves this must remain confidential unless they disclose abuse or not sharing the information would place the young person at risk of significant harm.

- Pupils who have experienced homophobic bullying may require immediate support following an incident but they may well also need ongoing support to feel safe in your school.

- Role models should not be drawn solely from sources such as television or music. Who are the gay or lesbian positive role models in your school?

CHAPTER 9

Prevention

What do you see your school being 'for'? To teach children to pass examinations? To prepare them for the world of work? Or to ground them morally, ethically and socially as well as academically? Do your senior leadership colleagues and your governors or trustees share your vision for your school?

The fact of the matter is that not all of our pupils are having their educational needs met. Some are suffering because of homophobic bullying and accordingly their schoolwork is paying a similar price. There will be a pupil or pupils leaving your school this academic year who did not thrive. They had a wretched time convinced that we were not there to help them. It is so easy to cater for the high-achieving pupils who not only reward us with the evidence of their intelligence or talent but can articulate so readily how we have helped them. The ones it is an effort to support demand more of us but not doing so means we 'lose' pupils: either actually because they leave the school or we lose their potential. They become frustrated and their parents too because despite all the responsibility and nurturing they invest at home they do not see this reflected in their child's schooling:

> 'I watched my handsome, witty, confident boy become ill with the constant abuse. He became physically ill and run down. He was mentally battered with continuous put-downs. He was very courageous to just set foot in that school day after day knowing what he would be facing. But not even the very

strongest could be expected to maintain any sort of self-worth under those circumstances. Eventually he calmly declared he would rather be dead than have to face that another day.' Clair, parent of a homophobically bullied 13-year-old

It follows therefore that creating a positive and inclusive ethos where homophobic bullying is recognised in all its forms, and pupils feel safe and confident to report homophobic bullying, needs commitment throughout the entire school (see Figure 9.1). It requires everyone to purposefully promote the equality of gay and transgender people as part of a school ethos that celebrates diversity and challenges all forms of inequality.

The answer to challenging homophobic bullying is preventing it in the first place. At the heart of prevention must be a positive school ethos where pupils and staff treat one another with respect because they know this is the right way to behave. This positive ethos must be promoted as soon as anyone joins your school and walks through its gates.

Your school may be engaging in good practice in relation to celebrating diversity and challenging inequality on the grounds of race, faith, gender or disability but the legacy of the UK's Section 28 has historically stifled the promotion of gay equality in school. Despite this, recognising gay equality does not require reinventing the wheel. Schools with an established ethos of celebrating diversity of any kind will already have the mechanisms in place to begin celebrating diversity of all kinds. Building a positive and inclusive school culture demands a combination of senior leadership, effective school policies, robust staff training, targeted initiatives and inclusive curriculum opportunities.

Have we collected data about homophobic bullying via surveys and informal methods? **No** Collect data. This will refine the strategies to be developed and then help monitor and evaluate them.

 Yes

Does the data indicate that homophobic bullying exists in our school? **No** Are we using the right systems for collecting data? Have we asked pupils about their experiences?

 Yes

Have we shared our findings with the governors?

Do they understand the impact of homophobic bullying on our school? **No** The governors are important allies and have a statutory responsibility to implement anti-bullying policies. Governors need to understand the impact of homophobic bullying so they can help develop inclusive policies to tackle it.

 Yes

Have we written to parents about our findings, explained that homophobic bullying can affect all pupils, and indicated that policies will change to reflect this? **No** Parents may think that preventing homophobic bullying means encouraging pupils to be gay. It does not. We must help them understand this.

 Yes

Have we informed all staff (paid and unpaid) about our findings?

Do they understand the impact that homophobic bullying has on attainment?

Do they feel committed to tackling it? **No** Staff may not prevent homophobic bullying if they do not understand it, or recognise the effect that it has on pupils. They will also feel more confident about doing so if they have the backing of the leadership team.

Yes

Do pupils understand that homophobic bullying will not be tolerated in our school? Have we used tutorial time, policies and other opportunities (such as curriculum) to tell them this in an age-appropriate way? **No** Pupils will continue to bully others in a homophobic way if they are not told that it is wrong. Pupils who experience homophobic bullying will be less likely to come forward.

Figure 9.1 Raising awareness about homophobic bullying in the school
Adapted from DCSF (2007)

Senior leadership

Securing the support of senior members of staff such as your headteacher and the governors is essential to ensuring that a positive and inclusive culture is reflected in a school's day-to-day work. Not only are senior leaders responsible for developing policies and procedures in line with government guidance and legislation, they should also ensure that such developments are undertaken in collaboration with pupils, parents, staff and governors.

On top of this, senior leaders should support the professional development of staff by ensuring that everyone understands the policies and procedures in place and has access to appropriate training. As employers they are also responsible for ensuring staff are not discriminated against on the grounds of sexual orientation. Therefore headteachers and governors have a duty both to ensure that staff are able to challenge homophobic bullying and feel protected from it too.

School policies

Developing a set of inclusive policies helps to ensure your school's values are communicated clearly as well as understood and enacted by all members of your school (see Figure 9.2). Pertinent policies are ones related to behaviour, anti-bullying, equal opportunities, safeguarding, e-safety, staffing and school improvement. Such policies should be working documents which communicate expectations to the whole school. Once again any changes to policies should be conducted in consultation with pupils, parents and staff.

It is important to remember that bullying will never be eradicated in schools if policies which are both consulted upon and 'owned' by the entire school are not put into place.

Teachers are far less likely to challenge inappropriate behaviour in their pupils if policies are absent, inadequate, 'unplugged' or the only move towards a 'whole school approach to challenging homophobic bullying' amounts to an ad hoc assembly and sticking up a poster telling pupils to 'get' themselves 'over' people being gay.

Policies should make explicit reference to homophobic bullying alongside other forms of prejudice-based bullying and behaviours. They should also recognise that this form of bullying can happen online as well as offline. Linking policies also helps create a clear and consistent message and demonstrates that bullying is part of a 'continuum of behaviour' rather than something separate (Ofsted, 2012, p.13). Further information about developing your school's anti-bullying policy can be found in Chapter 10.

| Does our governors' written statement of general principles for our behaviour policy make reference to bullying and homophobic bullying? | **No** ▶ | Look at our key policies that shape responses to bullying. Can they be more inclusive? |

▼ **Yes**

| Is homophobic bullying referenced in our anti-bullying policies and procedures? | **No** ▶ | Staff and pupils will not necessarily presume that a generic policy includes homophobic bullying. |

▼ **Yes**

| Have we conducted an audit of all other policies and procedural areas such as curriculum, safeguarding and e-safety? | **No** ▶ | Preventing homophobic bullying can be achieved in a variety of contexts. It is not just a specific response to an incident. Explore all opportunities. |

▼ **Yes**

| Have we consulted governors, parents, other staff and pupils about changes to policies? Consultation can help increase buy-in and counteract future criticism. | **No** ▶ | Consultation will make our policies more effective and help achieve their implementation. |

▼ **Yes**

| Have we looked at existing anti-bullying strategies to see if they can be developed to include homophobic bullying? | **No** ▶ | Homophobic bullying does not necessarily need a completely new approach. Using existing mechanisms and methods can be equally effective. |

▼ **Yes**

| Have we told other agencies about the progress we are making? Have we shared our experiences with the local authority and other schools? | **No** ▶ | Sharing knowledge helps others to prevent homophobic bullying and enables our school to feel proud of its achievements. |

Figure 9.2 Developing policies, practices and procedures
Adapted from DCSF (2007)

Staff training

Anti-bullying measures are most effective when every staff member understands the principles and purpose of the school's policy, its legal responsibilities regarding bullying, how to resolve problems and where to seek support (see Figure 9.3). Staff training therefore has a vital role to play in preventing homophobic bullying. It is important that staff develop an understanding of how prejudice-based bullying differs from general bullying so that they acquire the skills to respond to and challenge the underlying prejudices. Box 9.1 contains a case study of how staff training helped inspire a South Gloucestershire school's practice around homophobic bullying.

Staff training should not only ensure that your colleagues can respond to the prejudiced-based behaviour of others but prompt them to reflect too on their own attitudes and role in reinforcing or shaping the possible prejudices of our pupils. Staff can play a crucial role in perpetuating homophobic bullying: either by harbouring their own prejudices or failing to challenge homophobic behaviour. This should never be underestimated.

Staff training should not start and end with teachers. It is important to also include learning mentors, teaching assistants, lunchtime supervisors, site managers and administrative staff. All staff should understand school policies and their responsibility for upholding and modelling a positive and inclusive school culture.

Box 9.1 Bradley Stoke Community School – Good As You

At Bradley Stoke Community School we felt that having EACH work with us on delivering training on homophobic bullying to staff was a key factor in ensuring that everyone thought about their personal responsibility as part of the bigger whole school picture. The training was met with overwhelmingly positive feedback and staff were motivated and inspired to establish a consistent approach to tackling homophobic language use. As a school we agreed that doing this in a non-confrontational way which challenged inappropriate language whilst seeking to inform and educate was a preferred route. The staff team felt empowered to work together and were clear that any persistent issues would need a more consequence-based approach. What was particularly interesting was that students had a really broad range of views about how they wanted the school to tackle issues of inappropriate language use. These ranged from detentions and exclusion to the death penalty! It was clearly a very emotive topic and the student voice was very strongly telling us that they wanted us to take action where it was needed.

In February 2013 we launched our 'Good As You' focus week. We took the word 'gay' and created staff t-shirts with the slogan 'Good As You'. The vast majority of staff wore these for the entire focus week and it caused a great deal of interest amongst students. To back up this message, all assemblies for this week focussed on the results of their anonymous survey and challenged student attitudes to the words they sometimes used. This approach was very successful. Conversations between staff and students showed that we were making an impact and making them think about the words they were using. For us, however, this wasn't just about having a focus week; it was about starting to build the foundations where young people feel safe and secure to simply be themselves.

We see this work as just the beginning and have already started making plans for our next phase which aims to develop a staff and student equal opportunities forum: a champion group for all students who may feel 'different' because of their background, sexual orientation, ethnicity or religion. We have planned to ask EACH to support us with this by providing training for student volunteers who can act as mentors to other young people in school, and we will be exploring the use of technology to support students who may find face-to-face conversations difficult.

As a school we thread positive attitudes about celebrating difference, tolerance and diversity throughout the curriculum and in everything we do as a staff team. Our work in making sure that students feel confident that other students will not bully or intimidate them because they are a young gay, lesbian, bisexual or transgender student is part of a continuing journey for us and we are grateful for the continued support from EACH.

Teachers and wider school staff play a number of roles throughout the school day and move between them imperceptibly and continuously, e.g. educator, nurse, warden, counsellor, parent, confidante, custodian and advocate (DeWitt, 2012). This is especially noticeable where positive role models are absent from a pupil's home life. Teachers can often be the only source of comfort and security to gay pupils and it should never be underestimated what value they place on the psychological and physical refuge provided by a caring, interested teacher, learning support assistant (LSA) or mentor. Memories of and gratitude towards such adults remain with a gay person their entire life. Unfortunately not every school offers such support and pupils remain feeling anxious and very alone.

Do our staff understand the purpose of the anti-bullying policy and their responsibilities? → **No** → Staff will not be able to prevent homophobic bullying if they do not understand the general policies about bullying.

Yes ↓

Do our staff understand, feel motivated and confident that they can intervene to prevent homophobic bullying? → **No** → If staff lack confidence in responding to incidents of homophobic bullying, they are likely to let incidents pass without intervening.

Yes ↓

Do our staff know how to talk to young people experiencing homophobic bullying? Have they been trained to respond appropriately to young people in secondary schools who are lesbian, gay or bisexual? → **No** → If a staff member responds inappropriately to a pupil they will feel unsupported, will be unlikely to report any future incidents and become 'at risk'.

Yes ↓

Do our staff know how to support pupils who are experiencing homophobic bullying but are not gay? Do they understand that this may require a different response? → **No** → A pupil may not tell anyone they are experiencing homophobic bullying if they think our teachers will think they are gay. Staff need to be trained to ask sensitive questions.

Yes ↓

Are all our staff, including student and agency teachers and unpaid staff, aware that homophobic bullying is unacceptable in school and that they should intervene? → **No** → Staff often lack confidence about intervening in cases of homophobic bullying. All new staff need to be explicitly told they should intervene and know how to do this.

Yes ↓

Do all our staff feel protected from homophobic bullying and know that they will have the full support of the leadership team if they experience it? → **No** → Staff who do not feel safe at school will not want to stay and will not be as effective in the classroom. Staff need to know that they are supported regardless of their sexual orientation.

Figure 9.3 Steps for staff development
Adapted from DCSF (2007)

Targeted initiatives

Targeted initiatives provide an opportunity to reinforce a positive and inclusive school culture (see Box 9.2). This can include awareness days, workshops, sign-posting and drop-in sessions as well as involving the wider neighbourhood and utilising a variety of organisations. Various calendar opportunities exist throughout the year for these initiatives such as Anti-Bullying Week (coordinated by the Anti-Bullying Alliance), Safer Internet Day, LGBT History Month in February, the USA's Day of Silence and the International Day Against Homophobia and Transphobia (IDAHOT) on 17 May every year.

> **Box 9.2** Worle Community School Anti-Bullying Fortnight
>
> Each year in November, Worle Community School hosts an anti-bullying month to coincide with national Anti-Bullying Week and to spotlight the work of the school to challenge all forms of bullying. During anti-bullying month 2013 pupils from the house council worked with EACH to utilise activities from its Reach Teaching Resource and prevent homophobic bullying at Worle Community School. Teachers across the school were asked to deliver a range of activities with their pupils from the Resource exploring homophobic and cyberbullying. Following the activities pupils completed a survey evaluating the impact of the work on homophobic bullying with 85 per cent of pupils indicating they had developed a better understanding of homophobic bullying and 86 per cent stating they would now report homophobic bullying as a result of the anti-bullying month.

Schools do not have to be restricted to embarking on targeted initiatives within these months if it does not suit their programme. In fact delimiting discussion of gay equality or discrimination issues (and particularly homophobic or transphobic bullying) solely to preordained calendar dates misses numerous opportunities for 'teachable moments' such as what is topical in the news. Members of staff with a connection to personal, social, health and economic

education or a pastorally related role such as link teacher to the
school council or similar can capitalise upon topical and timely
'teachable moments' as they arise.

A perfect example is the introduction of the first same-sex
marriages at midnight on 29 March 2014 in the UK. The UK's
Channel 4 News ran a nightly 'magazine' piece all that week on
what it means to be gay in 2014: 'We are so gay'. Opportunities
such as these arise frequently and give you lots to discuss with your
pupils.

Curriculum opportunities

Raising awareness about issues regarding equality and diversity
through the curriculum is key to preventing and challenging
homophobic bullying as it provides opportunities for pupils to
understand, reflect upon and challenge their own prejudice. Box 9.3
contains a case study of a school with whom EACH worked since
2005 that covers gay and transgender equality in its curriculum
on a regular basis. Schools should make time in the curriculum
to promote equal opportunities, enable pupils to challenge
discrimination and stereotyping and introduce them to the concept
that any kind of bullying is morally wrong and illegal in the
workplace (see Figure 9.4). It is also important that the curriculum
meets the needs of its gay pupils. Schools should be mindful not to
make assumptions about the sexual orientation of its pupils, their
families or its staff in the delivery of lessons and ensure all strands
of diversity including sexuality and gender identity are covered in
lessons.

Subjects such as PSHE, citizenship, sex and relationship
education or religious education provide good opportunities
to explore equality and diversity. To truly embed a positive and
inclusive culture there needs to be a strong emphasis on ensuring
that pupils are able to extend and apply their learning to a range
of subjects.

Teachable moments in addition to those previously mentioned
include challenging use of the word 'gay' when used insultingly
or disparagingly, opening up a debate for instance about Russian

President Putin's views about same-sex relationships and attitudes towards this or the Gay Games choosing 'That's So Gay' as its campaign slogan featuring lesbian, gay or bisexual athletes. Later, this can lead to wider discussion about human rights and an exploration of countries around the world in which same-sex relationships are illegal. Pupils need to see gay and transgender equality and rights in the context of other rights movements: women, BME or disability. Pupils cannot be expected to understand how, in the UK, it has taken until 2014 to see the introduction of same-sex marriage simply by telling them to focus on contemporaneous fact ('Well, gay people can get married now. Get over it') and not explain the lead-up to this via historical context.

Schools should aim to use language which is gender neutral. Exploring with your pupils the etymology of words and how societal power is very much mixed in with our gendered vocabulary will be illuminating and fascinating to many pupils. Ask the girls why they are happy to be addressed as 'you guys' when part of a mixed-sex group whilst boys in a mixed group would baulk instantly at being referred to as 'dolls' (whilst the girls would fall about laughing). Why are male members of staff in schools referred to as 'Sir' whilst the female ones always 'Miss'? I recently worked with a school where female teachers are called 'Madam' to accurately reflect how an adult would address a woman with whose name they were unfamiliar or in a professional context.

Masculine words, sports, pastimes and jobs continue to have greater status than feminine ones. You might want to discuss in PSHE, citizenship, history, English or modern foreign languages the implications of the feminisation of words ending in 'ette' (cigarette, statuette, leatherette): it reduces their status from the masculine to indicate a lower value or worth. You could similarly debate 'landlady' compared with 'landlord' or 'manageress' versus 'manager'. Two fantastic books on the sexism in the English language which have more than stood the test of time include *Boys Don't Cry: Boys and Sexism in Education* and *Language and Gender* (Askew and Ross, 1988; Goddard and Patterson, 2000).

Box 9.3 Wyedean School LGBT week

During LGBT week at Wyedean School Year 8 students have the opportunity to focus on a range of related topics that encourage them to consider the impact of prejudice both at school and in wider society. The week aims to raise the profile of Wyedean School's commitment to equality and make it an even greater community in which students can work and learn.

The Year 8 LGBT week engages younger students on these issues through the use of lessons, assemblies and tutorials. During the week, subject teachers encourage reflection on a variety of related topics ranging from current attitudes towards same-sex relationships, a celebration of the groundbreaking contributions made to our society by LGBT people (for example Alan Turing) and the importance of language in our day-to-day conduct. The students also cover other important issues including attitudes to same-sex relationships and the terrible oppression suffered by LGBT people throughout history, as well as in countries around the world today. We also invite outside speakers including EACH to work with the students and staff, adding yet another dimension to the work. Wyedean School has worked with EACH since 2005.

It is great to see so many subjects and year groups getting involved to help raise awareness of our commitment to tackling homophobia and the reasons for it. The response from the Year 8s is really encouraging and the students are very willing to share what they have learned from the lessons, tutorials and their work with EACH. Their comments demonstrate a growing understanding of the importance of homophobic language, the impact it can have and their role in challenging it.

Recent school surveys at Wyedean evidence a significant fall in the amount of homophobic language being heard. This has been down to the proactive work done by a great number of staff, students and outside agencies. One of the key reasons for the success of the project concerns the way in which staff have embraced it and this is in no small part down to EACH's training input at inset sessions which puts our project's anti-homophobia drive firmly on the radar.

Have we reviewed the curriculum to identify opportunities to undertake anti-bullying work?	Bullying does not just have to be challenged in the context of responding to incidents. Teaching and learning about respect and tolerance is key to preventing bullying.

Yes ↓

Does our school curriculum make specific reference to homophobic bullying?	In so doing, our staff will be given greater confidence to challenge and prevent homophobic bullying and discrimination in an age-appropriate way. Explore all opportunities.

 No

Yes ↓

Does our senior leadership team understand that anti-bullying initiatives including homophobic bullying should be incorporated into our curriculum?	The curriculum in general provides lots of opportunities to talk about homophobic bullying and discrimination in an age-appropriate way. Explore all opportunities.

No

Yes ↓

Have we identified specific ways to include homophobic bullying in PSHE, citizenship and across the curriculum?	These areas provide explicit opportunities to discuss bullying and therefore should include homophobic bullying.

 No

Yes ↓

Have we identified other opportunities to discuss homophobic bullying such as class time, tutorial time and general discussions?	Tutorials and class time can all provide opportunities for pupils to raise issues and enter discussions. Teaching and learning about gay people needs to be age appropriate, but pupils should feel able to raise issues and discussions themselves in a variety of contexts.

 No

Yes ↓

Have we considered specific activities that could be undertaken if a pupil is experiencing bullying because they are gay themselves or have gay family members?	Schools should be able to respond quickly to support individuals in an appropriate helpful and sensitive way. Developing strategies for targeted work will be useful for staff.

 No

Figure 9.4 Developing the curriculum to prevent homophobic bullying
Adapted from DCSF (2007)

Key points

- Draw up through consultation and enshrine in practice comprehensive anti-bullying polices which make specific reference to homophobic bullying. Ensure each member of staff and every pupil knows how to access school policies (every school's PSHE policy should be on its website and there is no reason why your school's anti-bullying policy should not be there similarly).

- Let your school see that you deal as swiftly as possible with incidents of bullying, harassment or intimidation aimed at either pupils or staff.

- Speak and act confidently and positively when referring to or about sexuality issues around the school. Do not whisper 'gay' or 'lesbian' surreptitiously to colleagues in hushed tones as if you are talking about something clandestine. Other colleagues and pupils (the latter of whom intuit a great deal and often very accurately) will formulate opinions and draw relevant conclusions based on how you are seen to address issues of sexuality and gender identity.

- Identify and capitalise upon pupils' resilience and coping strategies. Much can be learnt from out gay pupils about their coping mechanisms. From this, good practice can be put in place and policies informed. Schools need to build on what is already being effectively implemented and moreover whatever works. Speak to your 'pupils with presence' here. Every school is different. If you have a friend who teaches in another school, with thriving 'out' gay pupils, invite them to come and speak to a year group in your school, or the staff or your school's LGBT Group or 'Gay Straight Alliance' (GSA) in the USA.

- Utilise every opportunity to flag up in school what is expected of everyone concerning equalities, respect, anti-discrimination work and prejudice-based bullying: use Facebook, Twitter (or whichever social media has now taken over from these!), posters on noticeboards, homework diaries, signs above reception, leaflets, blogs, newsletters, school prospectuses, z-cards (concertinaed fold-out cards) – the list is almost inexhaustible. Refresh the message continually so it remains contemporary, renewed, dynamic and appealing. This shows you are maintaining vigilance as a school on a number of levels.

CHAPTER 10

Anti-bullying Policies and Creating Inclusive Environments

Anti-bullying policies are the foundation upon which a safe and inclusive school environment is built. Effective policies should not only provide clear methods for dealing with reported or suspected cases of bullying but promote equality and diversity. It is vital, therefore, that these recognise all forms of prejudice-based bullying including homophobic bullying. Explicit references to homophobic bullying acknowledge it as a potential problem and provide staff with the tools to recognise and respond to it. These acknowledgements send a clear and authoritative message that homophobic bullying and name-calling will not be tolerated within your school.

Words alone however are not enough and your anti-bullying policy is only as successful as its implementation. The ethos of a policy must be embedded within the day-to-day practices of your school. For this to work a whole-school approach should be adopted. This means involving pupils, parents, staff, support staff, governors, trustees and other key stakeholders when developing and reviewing anti-bullying policies and procedures. Consulting with and including the whole school in the development of anti-bullying policies encourages everyone to take ownership of its implementation and establishes an inclusive culture from the outset whereby everyone's voice is valued and heard.

Anti-bullying policies can too often be subject to a 'copy and paste' or 'off the shelf' approach where example policies are adopted by schools. This approach is problematic as a single anti-bullying policy will not be applicable to the diverse school contexts in which it is being used. As a result policies conceived in this way will invariably reside on a dusty shelf unused and unread by the very people they are intended to support. Within the busy environment of a school it is understandable that such short-cuts appeal. I have been asked frequently since 2003 why a 'model policy' is not available to download from EACH's website and this is why. The development of an anti-bullying policy should not be viewed as simply an administrative exercise but an opportunity to engage the whole-school environment in a conversation about how to make the school a safe, welcoming and inclusive one for all.

Governors or trustees have legal responsibility for a school's anti-bullying policy and procedures. They should be able to demonstrate that policies have been regularly reviewed and developed in consultation at least with colleagues if indeed not with the pupils and staff of your school. If you are a governor with responsibility for behaviour or safeguarding it is important that you can evidence how this consultation process has been undertaken.

If you are a teacher who recognises an oversight with regard to homophobic bullying within your school's policies you can raise this with your manager. It can be useful to have evidence to present to them. This could include highlighting Ofsted's guidance on your school's actions to prevent homophobic bullying and keeping a record of incidents that have caused concern (Ofsted, 2014a). Together with your manager you can raise this issue with your senior leadership team.

If you are a parent and your school's anti-bullying policy does not explicitly reference homophobic bullying you should raise this as an issue with the school. You can talk through concerns with your child's teacher, tutor or head of year. Alternatively you may wish to write a letter to the headteacher. If these actions do not address your concerns you can send a letter to the Chair of Governors or Director of Trustees. If none of your interventions bring you satisfaction you may choose to write to either your local government ombudsman or to the Secretary of State for Education.

Developing an anti-bullying policy: the process

To ensure key stakeholders are represented from the outset, establish a working group to review current policies and procedures. The working group may include governors, members of the senior leadership team, LSAs, teachers, pupils and parents. It may also be advisable to invite an external agency with specialist and professional expertise around homophobia and cybersafety to brief the group. This will ensure the working group is appropriately resourced to address the issue of offline and online homophobic bullying within policies and procedures.

The working group should consult the whole school in order to establish:

- a common definition of bullying including homophobic bullying

- an understanding of the extent and types of bullying that occur and where

- opportunities for reporting incidents

- expected roles and responsibilities of staff, governors, parents and pupils

- a hierarchy of sanctions to prevent and respond to bullying

- a reward system to reinforce and celebrate positive behaviour.

These discussions will inform the core of your anti-bullying policy, establishing a common understanding of bullying and how it should be dealt with by the school.

Consulting staff

Staff need to be informed and on board with developments to anti-bullying policies and procedures if they are to implement them effectively. In a 2012 study, Ofsted found that senior leadership teams had an 'overly positive' view of their colleagues' understanding and confidence with regards to homophobic bullying (Ofsted, 2012, p.37). Your colleagues can be confident they are addressing these issues by completing questionnaires and training needs assessments. These should not be issued to teaching staff alone but also capture the insights of learning mentors, teaching assistants, lunchtime supervisors, site managers and administrative staff. Support staff are equally vital for ensuring the ethos of your school's policy is embedded within day-to-day practice and for modelling an inclusive school culture.

A staff questionnaire or training needs assessment could cover:

- perspectives on homophobic bullying in your school and how prevalent they feel it is

- understanding of different aspects of homophobic bullying such as who experiences it, who perpetrates it and what it looks like

- experience of dealing with homophobic bullying and how well they felt they dealt with it

- any barriers they have identified in challenging homophobic bullying, for example this could be linked to their own professional confidence, personal convictions, difficulty engaging with parents or problematic school procedures

- knowledge of lesbian and gay issues and supporting sensitive disclosures

- what works, positive experiences and examples of best practice that they have witnessed in your school or others.

Analysing results from your staff consultation will help identify gaps in knowledge. It may be, for example, that teachers recognise homophobic language where it occurs but do not feel equipped to challenge it, do not recognize it or do not acknowledge it as an issue. Once you have identified areas that need attention staff training can be tailored to meet these specific needs. Tapping into EACH or another training provider's expertise to deliver staff training can be particularly helpful for motivating and inspiring staff to establish a consistent approach to homophobic bullying.

Consulting pupils

Pupils are vital to the success of anti-bullying strategies and their voice should be at the heart of interventions. For anti-bullying initiatives to be a success schools must establish a reporting culture whereby pupils feel confident that they can tell someone about their bullying and secure the support they need. Too often pupils fear that the bullying will not be dealt with and telling someone will only make the problem worse. If pupils are not confident that the procedures in place will be effective then more work needs to be done by the school to instil this confidence. Reviewing anti-bullying policies and procedures on a regular basis will provide an opportunity to reflect on whether this is the case in your school and identify areas for improvement.

There are a multitude of opportunities with which to consult over anti-bullying strategies. These include:

- staff focus groups

- face-to-face discussions with small groups of pupils across the year groups such as the school council

- exploring the topic in PSHE, citizenship, politics, general studies or SRE

- completing anonymous feedback forms and questionnaires.

Little Mead Primary Academy in Bristol, UK has a visionary headteacher whom I have known for over 25 years. Barbara Daykin addresses issues of equality and diversity with her primary age pupils and staff continuously. She wanted her school to revise its anti-bullying policy so she invited one of the school's governors and EACH to work with small groups of children drawn from Reception to Year 6 (from the first to the final year of elementary school), appraising the existing policy and drafting wording for the new one in their own words. Understandably, the ultimate policy was couched in a register reflecting the top end of the primary school rather than the youngest year but what a fantastic way to include all ages of children at a grass roots level and what a thrill for those children to be selected to participate. They will remember this always and we hope they will hold on to the laudable reasons why the school wanted to do things this way. An illustration of part of Little Mead Primary Academy's anti-bullying policy is available in Box 10.1.

Box 10.1 'Say No To Bullying'

Purpose

At Little Mead Primary School we promote the values of honesty, respect and a sense of community. We believe that every child matters and aim that all children will:

- **Be successful, resilient and ambitious learners.**
- **Be respectful and responsible local and global citizens.**
- **Have the aspiration, confidence and skills to continue learning beyond school.**

One way in which we pursue these aims, is through our positive approach to Anti Bullying. In school we call this strategy **'Say No to Bullying'**.

If children are to understand that bullying is wrong and to have the confidence to say no to bullying, they need to be able to empathise, or 'stand in the shoes' of others. They need to be able to form good relationships and understand how to deal with conflict. They should understand that they have rights, but also that they have responsibilities.

We are committed to providing a caring, friendly and safe environment where pupils can learn and participate in all aspects of school life. We value the self esteem of every child. Everybody has the right to be treated with respect and bullying of any kind is unacceptable.

If bullying does occur, all pupils should be able to tell an adult. We will respond promptly and effectively to issues of bullying. Pupils who bully must take responsibility for their actions and need to learn different ways of behaving.

What Is Bullying?
The following definitions have been discussed and agreed by staff, parents and pupils:

- Bullying is the use of aggression or coercion with the intention of hurting another person. Bullying is the repeated use of these things, causing distress and anxiety to the victim.

- Bullying is unkindness which you don't like and which hurts you. It is continuous and may carry on even after an adult has intervened.

Bullying can be:

Emotional:	Unfriendly, excluding, tormenting or threatening. 'Ganging up'
Verbal:	Name-calling, sarcasm, spreading rumours, teasing
Physical:	Pushing, kicking, hitting, punching or any use of violence
Racist:	Racial taunts, graffiti, gestures
Homophobic:	Focussing on sexuality
Cyber:	Email and internet chat room misuse, threats by text messaging and calls

Talking to pupils will also help your school identify pockets of excellence along with areas of practice that need attention. You can ask pupils about situations in which a response to homophobic bullying or language was felt to be particularly effective. Similarly if approaches to challenging homophobic bullying are inconsistent across the school your 'pupils with presence' can tell you. You may consider working with pupils to establish a hierarchy of sanctions and rewards to deter negative behaviour and celebrate positive behaviour. This will promote a just, fair culture and pupils will be less likely to take umbrage over a sanction that they themselves designed.

Another added benefit of consulting pupils is that they will be able to alert you to any issues arising before they become full-blown problems. Problematic behaviour online, for example, may only come to the attention of your school if it escalates into a safeguarding issue. Consulting pupils about what they do online will proactively prevent such issues arising and allow you to understand how your pupils view and manage their own safety and wellbeing. As previously mentioned, North Somerset Council issued an anonymous authority-wide survey to pupils in 2014 asking for their opinion about what matters to them and how the Council and its schools could improve. The survey was adapted for younger pupils in Years 6 and 7 and older pupils in Year 8 and above. Questions covered the following topics:

- what pupils do in their spare time and how safe they feel when engaging in these activities

- if pupils feel that their views are listened to and valued within the school

- the extent to which the school provides information about healthy lifestyles, including appropriate sex and relationship education

- how they feel about bullying, whether they have experienced it and how well they think their school deals with it, including specific questions about homophobic bullying

- if they use social media, how often and in what ways.

Consulting parents

Parents need to be consulted and feel their opinions are valued when developing school policies and procedures. This can be especially important when developing practice around a sensitive topic such as homophobic bullying. Parents are important allies to ensuring an inclusive school culture is promoted both inside and outside of school. This requires clear and effective communication with them to ensure they are informed of school developments.

Engaging parents can be a challenge for many schools. It is a fact that the less positive a parent's experience of their own schooling the less likely they are to engage with your school via their child. Primary schools will find that their parents are more involved with the school. Secondary schools often struggle to maintain this engagement however as pupils become older and more independent. There are numerous behavioural and academic benefits to continuing to engage parents with their child's school. Ofsted increasingly look at how schools are engaging pupils' and parents' views particularly when developing e-safety strategies (Ofsted, 2014b).

Response rates to parental consultations can be variable especially if parents do not feel their opinions are valued. Parents should feel trusted and listened to by the school and a variety of techniques can be employed to open up these channels of communication. Typical avenues include formal parent-teacher meetings and annual or biennial surveys. These opportunities can be further promoted through letters home, newsletters, text messages, email reminders, social media call outs and prize draws. These methods should not only be used to elicit parental views but also feed back to parents about the findings of consultations. Regardless of whether messages are positive or critical you should be willing to discuss results with your school and provide detailed plans of action. This will demonstrate to parents and the school more widely that their views were listened to and the school is taking proactive action. This not only helps build better relationships between your school and its parents but may encourage parents to offer their specific expertise or support to anti-bullying working groups.

A number of parents at the school may be lesbian, gay or bisexual and will need and wish to feel represented within your policies and procedures. Utilising inclusive language within general school communications is a great opportunity to demonstrate that all parents are valued 'family members' of the school. Actively invite lesbian or gay parents to join your school's board of governors or trustees. This will send a positive and powerful message to the entire school about how much you value different families. Your school will gain hugely from an informed, articulate gay parent.

Writing the policy

Schools should involve the whole school in agreeing the definition of bullying so that the issue is understood and owned by everybody. Your school's definition should be suitably child friendly and accessible according to the age and ability of the pupils. Box 10.2 outlines a structure that could be used for an anti-bullying policy.

Be clear on the audience for your policy. It may be necessary to develop a suite of differentiated policies that are accessible and workable documents for governors, teaching staff, pupils and parents.

Promoting the policy

Once the anti-bullying policy has been published ensure that you promote it widely and celebrate the achievements of those who contributed to its formation. You can communicate and disseminate the anti-bullying policy across the school by:

- discussing it with pupils during tutorial time

- assigning dedicated staff training to the new policy and what it means for school practice

- informing parents of the policy via parent-teacher meetings or school newsletters.

In order to celebrate the achievements of those involved in creating the policy and to ensure it is promoted with some fanfare, host an anti-bullying launch involving the whole school. This will help elevate the policy and the valuable work that has gone into creating it. Celebrating the success helps affirm your school's positive ethos and assures everyone that everybody at the school is valued and equal.

Box 10.2 Anti-bullying policy

Purpose
Make a positive and inclusive statement about the school and that bullying will not be tolerated.

Definition
Agree a common and accessible definition of bullying with your pupils. Remember to include details of types of bullying behaviour. For example physical, verbal, relational or material. Also include details of types of prejudice based bullying such as homophobic, racist and disablist.

Reporting bullying
Explain to pupils what they should do if they are a target of bullying or they witness bullying. Also explain how they can expect school staff to respond should they report an incident of bullying and detail the hierarchy of sanctions in place for bullying incidents.

It may also be apposite to include information for parents here on what they can do if their child is being bullied. Alternatively this can be issued as a supplementary document.

Recording bullying
Include a statement about confidentiality here along with details of where bullying reports will be recorded and who is responsible for this system. You should also explain how this information will be used so pupils understand why the information is being recorded.

Strategies for preventing bullying
Explain the initiatives and strategies in place at the school to prevent bullying from occurring and to promote an inclusive ethos.

Key points

- Anti-bullying policies are the bedrock of work in challenging homophobic bullying and building safe and inclusive school environments.

- The ethos of a policy must be embedded within the day-to-day practices of the school.

- Everyone in the school should be consulted when developing an anti-bullying policy, not least its pupils.

- Be clear on the audience for your policy ensuring it is accessible and relevant for governors, teaching staff, pupils and parents.

- Celebrate the policy at every opportunity and review it regularly to ensure procedures are effective and up to date.

CHAPTER 11

Frequently Asked Questions

1. What is homophobia?

Homophobia is a resentment or fear of lesbian, gay and bisexual people. At its most benign it is voiced as a passive dislike of gay people. At its worst it involves active victimisation: targeting an individual in direct or indirect ways. Homophobia can also affect people perceived to be lesbian, gay or bisexual, someone who has an association with gay people or someone who does not conform to stereotypical expectations of masculine or feminine behaviour.

2. What is transphobia and what is the difference between transgender and transsexual?

Transphobia describes the aggression or negativity directed at a transgender man, woman, boy or girl. This can range from jokes, graffiti, insults and threats to physical attacks. **Transgender** is the umbrella term for people who identify with a gender other than that assigned to them at birth. Not all transgender people undergo medical interventions. The term can be acceptably abbreviated to 'trans'.

Transsexual is the medical term for someone whose sense of gender differs from their biological sex, for example someone whose biological sex is male but who identifies as a woman. Most people who identify as transsexual have had surgery to align their biological sex with their psychological gender. This is a gender reassignment or gender alignment. A pupil or teacher at your school who has undergone gender reassignment surgery will invariably refer to themselves as a boy/man or a girl/woman or 'trans' – not as a 'post-operative transsexual'! Avoid any reference to the term 'sex change'.

3. What is homophobic bullying or harassment?

Just like any form of bullying or harassment, homophobia can be **direct** such as name-calling or physical assault or **indirect** such as spreading rumours or writing offensive graffiti. It can also be conducted online or via mobile devices. This is known as cyberbullying. Individuals or groups can be affected specifically if they are lesbian, gay or bisexual, thought to be by others or have a gay family member. What makes it different from other forms of bullying or harassment is the personal motivation and prejudice which drives it.

4. Why does homophobic bullying happen?

Homophobia in young people is the fear of and the reaction to gay people often people who do not conform to gender norms. People can have little understanding of these identities and simply be reacting to someone seen as 'different'.

Most prejudice-based bullying takes place at a time when young people are unsure of their own developing identity. It often reflects an anxiety within young people as we continually receive confusing messages from society about what it means to be 'a man' or 'a woman' and stereotypes of what it means to be gay, lesbian or bisexual.

5. Who gets homophobically bullied or harassed?

Anyone can become a target of homophobic bullying or harassment regardless of sexual orientation. You will find however that the following are common reasons why someone may be targeted:

- Young people may have misjudged their best friend by confiding in them only to find themselves 'outed' before they are ready.

- Heterosexual girls and boys who others think are gay are often taunted based on stereotypes about what it means to be gay.

- Young people who do not conform to ideas about how girls and boys should behave are often singled out.

- Friends of lesbian, gay or bisexual people are frequently forced to face up to their own prejudices, fears and preconceptions whilst finding themselves targets 'by association'.

- Young people with a gay parent or sibling can become targets.

6. Is homophobia a major issue?

Research in the UK and the USA regularly highlights that homophobic and transphobic abuse is all too common. In the UK a survey of 7000 lesbiam, gay, bisexual or transgender young people aged 16–25 years (METRO Youth Chances, 2014) found that:

- three in four have experienced name-calling

- one in two has experienced harassment and threats

- one in four has experienced physical assault.

In the USA a survey of 8,584 lesbian, gay, bisexual or transgender and heterosexual young people aged 13 to 20 (Kosciw, et al., 2012) found that:

- 82 per cent were verbally harassed in the past year because of their sexual orientation

- 38 per cent had experienced physical bullying because of their sexual orientation

- 55 per cent had experienced homophobic cyberbullying.

7. Is being gay the problem?

It is not being gay that makes some young people unhappy. It is the negative reaction of other people that they fear and coming to terms with being 'different' and coping with it that is difficult. It is even harder if this has to be done in secrecy from family, friends and teachers.

Gay people of all ages can find themselves emotionally exhausted by having to reconcile how they feel inside with the problems others have in coming to terms with their sexuality.

8. Is it appropriate to tell 'out' pupils, 'effeminate' boys or 'masculine' girls to be more discreet to avoid bullying?

No. Telling a pupil to be more discreet suggests the bullying is their fault, they are 'bringing it on themselves' and undermines their identity. Removing the target rather than responding to the bullying itself will not solve the problem. Schools need to work with pupils who engage in homophobic bullying to ensure they understand their behaviour is unacceptable, the impact of their actions, and to make amends for the damage caused. Pupils experiencing bullying need to be worked with to help them develop coping strategies and resilience.

9. But will I need to talk about their sexual activity when challenging homophobic bullying?

Addressing homophobic bullying and sexual orientation equality does not mean discussing sex. It means taking decisive and assertive action to prevent bullying and promote equality. Sexual orientation is distinct from sexual behaviour and refers to the combination of one's emotional, sexual and physical attraction to someone of the opposite, same or either sex. Neither heterosexual nor same-sex relationships are defined solely by sex. Just as schools are able to discuss heterosexual relationships without referring to sex it is equally possible to discuss same-sex relationships.

SRE has an important role to play in challenging many of the myths and misconceptions that underlie homophobic prejudice.

Under the Equality Act 2010 schools have a legal duty to ensure that teaching is accessible to all pupils including those who are lesbian, gay or bisexual. An SRE curriculum which includes inclusive and age-appropriate conversations about the emotional, social and physical aspects of same-sex relationships will complement and reinforce work in challenging homophobic bullying.

10. We have to respect cultural and religious differences. Does this mean pupils can be homophobic?

No. It is true that some religions or cultures are not as, or at all, inclusive or tolerant of same-sex relationships however this is never a justification for homophobic bullying. An individual has a right to believe what they want. It is unacceptable however for an individual to express their views in a way that degrades others. If a pupil engages in persistent bullying due to their cultural or religious traditions contacting their parents to alert them to the issue will be necessary and sanctions will be required.

There is a strong legal and moral imperative for educators to challenge homophobia whenever it occurs just as there is an imperative to challenge racist or faith-based prejudice wherever this occurs. Anyone can experience homophobic bullying regardless of their sexual orientation, religion, culture or national identity and all deserve to be protected. Educating pupils about our religious, cultural and national differences can be a great platform for celebrating diversity of all kinds. Respect, empathy and kindness should be integral to the ethos of every school.

11. I teach in a special school and my pupils are disabled or have additional needs. Is all of this relevant to them?

Too often pupils with additional or special educational needs (SEND) do not have their sexuality issues addressed and it is invariably assumed they are heterosexual. It is important however that these pupils have access to appropriate information, advice and guidance around sexual orientation and that teachers in special schools recognise that coming out support needs are differentiated proportionately for pupils with additional needs.

12. Is the phrase 'That's so gay' homophobic?

Over the years EACH has worked with many gay and heterosexual people who are upset and frustrated by the persistent use of 'gay' as a derogatory term. This use of language does not always equate to bullying as many young people use it to refer to an inanimate object or an unwelcome situation. Nevertheless, it is a 'micro-aggression', reinforcing on a daily basis the idea that being gay is somehow stupid, pathetic, rubbish or wrong. This language sends a very clear and negative message to gay young people and can make them feel worthless.

13. How does homophobic bullying differ from other forms of prejudice-based bullying?

Prejudice-based bullying is an umbrella term which refers to pupils being targeted because of who they are or who they are perceived to be. This can be on the grounds of race, faith, disability, gender, sexual orientation, gender identity or age. Homophobic bullying fits under the umbrella of prejudice-based bullying and all kinds of bullying differ in the motivations behind them and the way pupils experience this bullying. Homophobic bullying will be an expression of specific assumptions and prejudices as well as have different roots from other forms of prejudice-based bullying.

Pupils experiencing racist, faith-based, sexist and ageist bullying will frequently have family or friends who can relate to their experience. Identifying as gay can often make individuals feel 'invisible' and assume their family or friends will reject them if they find out they are gay. For similar reasons pupils who are not gay can fear others' assumption that they are. As a result homophobic bullying is one of the least reported forms of bullying as some pupils do not want aspersions cast on their sexual orientation.

14. I'm convinced some of our parents would be unhappy if we were to adopt an active stance against homophobic bullying. Should we?

No parent wants their child to be bullied, nor do most wish to hear that their child is a bully. Regardless of their views on gay people, or sexual orientation in general, parents need to recognise that your school has a legal responsibility to keep every pupil safe from harm. Preventing and responding to homophobic bullying are crucial if your school is to fulfil its responsibilities. Parents should be involved in your school's consultations on this topic and contribute to ways in which it can be stopped. Parents also need to acknowledge that any pupil can be affected by homophobic bullying: gay or heterosexual.

15. Primary school pupils do not know about gay people or understand sexual orientation. This isn't an issue for my primary school, surely?

I have taught and worked in hundreds of primary and secondary schools since 1985 and this has evidenced very clearly to me that the average seven-year-old understands that gay people 'exist' because they learn this from television or they have a brother, aunt, cousin, godparent or family friend who is lesbian or gay who they are quite happy to talk to you about if you wish them to. Primary school pupils will be too young to know their own sexual orientation but many will know someone who is gay. Homophobic language is used in our primary schools without our pupils necessarily understanding what it is that they are saying. If you are a primary school teacher, the same strategies you use to deal with other forms of inappropriate language you deploy here. Simply respond to homophobic language as you would when a child says something offensive but you know they do understand what they have said. Age-appropriately, you explain what is and is not acceptable in your school.

16. I am a teacher who happens to be gay. My pupils ask me questions about my sexuality. What am I allowed to say or not say?

Your school's ethos and staffroom culture will determine how open it wishes you to be about your sexual orientation and you would be advised to seek guidance from your headteacher in the first instance. The key is consistency and fairness amongst all staff regardless of sexual orientation. See Part Two 'Personal and Professional Conduct' in Teachers' Standards: Guidance for School Leaders, School Staff and Governing Bodies (DfE, 2013) for more information. Pupils, especially gay pupils, will benefit from knowing out, positive lesbian and gay role models. All staff should ensure that they provide advice and guidance objectively and without bias.

17. I am confident a pupil I teach is gay. Should I do anything about this?

There is no incumbency upon you to quiz any pupil about their sexual orientation or insinuate in your conversations with them that you are concerned that they may be gay. If a pupil chooses to come out to you it is important to be upbeat. That way, they will be more likely to tell you if they are concerned about anything including coming out or bullying. Developing a school ethos where all your pupils feel respected is essential to giving your pupils the assurance to talk to you if they need to.

18. We do not have any gay pupils at this school. Why would this be relevant?

You have, therefore it is. In an average sized high school of 1200 pupils at a conservative estimate, statistically 36 will identify as gay or bisexual in adulthood (even if only to themselves). Some will be coming out in a year or two's time and many will have same-sex relationships. What makes it relevant is that homophobic bullying can affect anyone regardless of sexual orientation. Anyone who is thought to be gay, or just thought to be different can be called gay or experience homophobic abuse. Even if a pupil is not gay, they may have close family members or friends who are and this is relevant to all of these pupils. Finally, there are gay people in the wider world (including, of course, the teachers in their school who may or may not be out) and therefore challenging homophobic bullying is essential to your pupils' wider education.

19. How should I treat the same-sex parent of a pupil in my school?

Like any other parent. Non-biological parents have the same rights and responsibilities as a step parent. These rights are enhanced if the same-sex parents are in a civil partnership or a same-sex marriage. It is important that schools treat non-biological parents in the same way as biological parents and they feel invited to be part of school life and activities. Some non-biological parents may apply to adopt a child. Some may apply for a parental responsibility order. This enables them to sign official forms from school, for example.

20. What about homophobic bullying outside of school?

Your school is partially responsible for bullying taking place outside school (including cyberbullying) in addition to taking steps to challenge bullying inside school. It must be responsive to incidents which happen when pupils are in uniform on their way to and from your school. This can be on foot or public transport or in local shops. Under the UK's Education and Inspection Act 2006 a school's behaviour policy can include measures to discipline poor behaviour both on and off school premises. See the *Behaviour and Discipline in Schools: Advice for Headteachers and School Staff* for more detail (DFE, 2014b).

CHAPTER 12

Last Words

In this final chapter I should like to leave you with some points upon which to reflect. They are informed by my years as a teacher, trainer and consultant working variously with teachers, the Department for Education (and its previous incarnations at home and overseas), schools, colleges and universities, Ofsted the Government Equalities Office, the major teaching unions, the police service, the College of Policing, the National Crime Agency (NCA; and its previous incarnations), the Crown Prosecution Service (CPS), the Prisons Service, the National Health Service, doctors, nurses, council officials, youth workers and others.

I distinctly remember my A level English teacher telling me, as we studied George Orwell's *1984*, that if we change the way we speak we change the way we think. I remain firmly convinced this is entirely true. The importance of adopting appropriate vocabulary when promoting equality and diversity cannot be understated. Language is a powerful tool. The way it is deployed reinforces stereotypes and inequality between groups. It also has the power to debunk such stereotypes, explode myths and expunge misconceptions.

So, here are some words, phrases and concepts upon which you may care to reflect as you pledge to undertake work around challenging homophobic bullying or supporting a young person who comes out to you as gay (or who is already out).

Heterosexual ¦ straight ¦ homosexual ¦ gay

Those who are in the majority in society enjoy a privileged social status – such as being heterosexual – and are invariably described in terms which reinforce such status. The word 'straight' to mean heterosexual is a classic example. 'Straight' means uniform, direct, level, upright and properly positioned. Whenever it is employed to refer to someone's heterosexuality it underpins their position as 'normal' and thus differentiates heterosexual people from those sexualities seen to be 'abnormal': bent, deviant, inverted or improper, i.e. bisexual, lesbian, gay.

It is this sense that gay people are 'abnormal' which leads some into the trap of talking about them as having sexual 'preferences', inclinations, proclivities or tendencies. We never, ever refer to heterosexual people as having an inclination, a proclivity or a tendency. Sexuality is similarly not like a box of chocolates with hard or soft centres for which you have a 'preference'. It is simply a fact!

The effect of this vocabulary is not only patronising and insulting but carries a number of implications. All three words refer to someone's predisposition to feel, act or behave in a certain way. When we refer to someone's 'homosexual tendencies' we often reduce gay people to certain feelings, actions and behaviours. These three words themselves carry innuendo, insinuating something is warped or 'out of true'. Heterosexual fits within the family of words describing sexual orientation and gender identity – heterosexual, lesbian, gay, bisexual and transgender – and which you will find used consistently by Government (local and national) and the Criminal Justice System. We can therefore avoid reductive language which 'does this' to lesbian, gay or bisexual people by using the words heterosexual and gay consistently.

Ironically, as I type this, a news story pops up from ynetnews. com's 'jewish world' (2014):

> **Gay haredim lead double life, survey shows** – Two-thirds of ultra-Orthodox homosexuals have chosen to marry women despite their sexual inclination, figures released by HOD organization, for religious homosexuals, reveal. Nearly half

of them admit they cheat on their wives with other men at least once a month.

In many instances the use, or as I see it misuse, of the word 'homosexual' (instead of gay) and indeed 'straight' instead of heterosexual arises from genuine ignorance about the genesis of words. As Thomas Rogers explains in his 'Salon' article published in 2012 – 'The invention of the heterosexual':

> 'Heterosexual' was coined the same time as the word 'homosexual' [in the mid-19th century], by an Austro-Hungarian journalist named Károly Mária Kertbeny. He created these words in response to Prussian legislation that made same-sex erotic behaviour illegal where the identical act performed by a man and a woman [was] legal. Trying to change legal opinion he coined 'heterosexual' and 'homosexual' in a very clever bid to equalize same-sex and different-sex. His intent was to suggest there are two categories in which human beings could be sexual and they were not part of a hierarchy.
>
> The term took a while to 'catch on' but did thanks to psychiatrists in the 1880s and 1890s: a part of the medical profession deeply unscientific at that time. It meant that somebody with a medical degree and all of the authority it brings could stand up and start making value judgments using specialized medical vocabulary and pass it off as authoritative and basically unquestionable.
>
> Psychiatry is responsible for creating the heterosexual in largely the same way that it is responsible for creating the various categories of sexual deviance that we are familiar with, recognize and define ourselves in opposition to. The period lasting from the late Victorian era to the first 20 or 30 years of the 20th century was a time of tremendous socioeconomic change. People desperately wanted to give themselves validity in this new world order. People established themselves as sexually normative. It wasn't, 'Oh, I'm a man and I like to sleep with other men, that makes me different,' creating this groundswell of change it was the men going, 'I'm not a degenerate, I don't want to sleep with other men, I am this

thing over here that is normative and acceptable and good and not pathological and right, that's what I am. I need people to understand that I am a valid person and need to be taken seriously'.

In the late 1800s and early 20th century social Darwinism [made it] important to prove that you were part of the solution and not part the problem. Authoritative medicalized ideas coming from very rarefied circles trickled into larger culture. Heterosexual simply became a synecdoche for normal. Freud talks about [attaining] heterosexuality. When you manage to develop yourself in the proper way, in an appropriate way, in the way that Freud says you're supposed to, what you end up with is a heterosexual.

And so homosexual effectively became stuck in aspic. Heterosexual has just one synonym – straight – to register society's approval of it. Compare this with the, literally, scores of synonyms for the word homosexual – most of which are deeply offensive and focus primarily on aggressive disapproval of 'the act'. Homosexual is an adjective deeply offensive to many, many gay men (and gay women – though 'homosexual' is rarely assigned to women) aware of the derivation of homosexual and heterosexual as explained above.

Gay community ¦ heterosexual community

We never, ever refer to the 'heterosexual community' so why do we refer to the 'gay community'? It always makes the speaker sound as if they are talking about a group of people to which they do not belong and who are uniform in their values and beliefs. From this it is a quick step to talking about 'gays' adopting the 'homosexual lifestyle', two other really unhelpful expressions. The police service uses 'the gay community' all the time and in my training and consultancy with police forces I encourage them to understand why expressions such as 'people who are gay' or 'individuals who are gay' are far more inclusive than 'gay community'.

When, at a conference at which we shared the same platform, I asked a black woman and a disabled gold medal-winning, female paralympian, 'Do you mind being referred to as members of the black and disabled community respectively?' they instantly and loudly voiced their antipathy towards these labels and stated that they were individuals and resented being 'all lumped together as members of some so-called community'. Interestingly, spontaneous applause erupted from the predominantly white, able-bodied, heterosexual audience.

Just gay

So often we see expressions in the tabloid press like 'openly gay' or 'admitting one is gay' like it is some sort of guilty secret to which one has confessed. Similarly, and perhaps the vocabulary is the result of the mindset brought about by their job as law enforcers, it is not uncommon for me to hear police officers in consultations or training I am delivering referring to targets of crime or its perpetrators as 'confessing to', 'admitting to' or 'owning up to' 'being gay'. This says quite a bit more about the police officer's awareness and attitude than perhaps they would care to acknowledge. Likewise it is never helpful to pluralise groups of people and describe them as Jews, the deaf, Muslims or gays, for example. It dehumanises people and makes any 'group' of people much easier to dismiss then demonise. Simply by adding 'people' after the noun demonstrates respect and accords people value: thus 'Jewish people' or 'people who are gay'. We are not defined by the element about us which is the subject of the sentence.

Target ¦ bully ¦ hate crime ¦ prejudice-based crime

I use 'target' consistently in my work, never 'victim'. A target is not necessarily hit. It can move. It can be missed. Victim has no synonym. It is a disempowering word with connotations of resignation and defeatism. Similarly, in my work with the Criminal Justice System I cringe whenever I hear individuals described as having been 'the victim of a hate crime'. Not all hate crimes are actually motivated by hate. Some arise from ignorance and lack of knowledge. Would a target of such a crime not feel so much more empowered about their situation were they to be described as having been 'the target of prejudice-based crime'? I believe so and I use this expression always because of this but also because in schools we talk about prejudice-based bullying not 'hate bullying'. Yet the adult phrase 'hate crime' (which we have imported from the USA) continues to be the one religiously barnacled onto by our Criminal Justice System. Once again, through my years of work with agencies from the NCA and College of Policing (as they are called today) to the CPS and police service, I can see positive headway having been made in fostering an awareness of the advantages of using language which appeals to targets of bullying or crime rather than victims of hate. Think therefore about using target instead of victim in your language describing bullying. It is bullying behaviour too which we are describing in our perpetrator. For this reason it is a really good idea not to call this girl or boy 'a bully'. The word 'bully' is like a sticker. It labels people as something. They are someone who, at the present time, bullies. What they do is demonstrate bullying behaviour. If we write them off as a bully they are far less likely to believe they can stop or bother trying.

One final thought – when we reduce people to TLAs (three letter abbreviations!) such as LGB it is too easy to stop thinking of them as people and certainly as individuals. Yes, it takes longer to say 'lesbian, gay or bisexual people' but it is definitely more inclusive and respectful. I notice similarly we are moving from BME (black and minority ethnic) as an abbreviation to BAME (black, Asian and minority ethnic). It is just something about which to open up a conversation with colleagues, friends and family as relevant.

Conclusion

Remember each of us has, as an adult, not only power and influence but also the moral duty to do what we can to challenge homophobic name-calling and bullying. I trust this book provides you with hands-on, practical guidance as to how to develop a holistic yet dynamic approach to this work, which until now has not been published.

Throughout the course of this book I have explored a range of topics and ideas which I hope will help you and your school better challenge and prevent homophobic bullying. This is an issue which has widespread impact on young people regardless of their sexual orientation and cannot be underestimated. Get this one right and you will definitely find other 'ist' forms of bullying (disablist/racist) becoming routinely easier to deal with. So, next time you hear a pupil in a corridor or your classroom say 'That's SO gay!' why not urge them to 'Use another word'? Or buy a dictionary. Best wishes.

Section 28 of the Local Government Act 1988

Section 28 of the Local Government Act 1988 was enacted to prevent local authorities from 'promoting homosexuality' and offering financial assistance to those 'promoting homosexuality'. The Section read as follows:

2A –

(1) A local authority shall not –

(a) intentionally promote homosexuality or publish material with the intention of promoting homosexuality;

(b) promote the teaching in any maintained school of the acceptability of homosexuality as a pretended family relationship;

(2) Nothing in subsection (1) above shall be taken to prohibit the doing of anything for the purpose of treating or preventing the spread of disease.

(3) In any proceedings in connection with the application of this section a court shall draw such inferences as to the intention of the local authority as may reasonably be drawn from the evidence before it.

(4) In subsection (1)(b) above 'maintained school' means –

(a) in England and Wales, a county school, voluntary school, nursery school or special school, within the meaning of the [Education Act 1996]; and

(b) in Scotland, a public school, nursery school or special school, within the meaning of the Education (Scotland) Act 1980.

As this provision is part of civil law, actions by local authorities can be challenged only by judicial review; usually an injunction or prohibiting order is issued to restrain the authority from continuing with its action.

The Bill received Royal Assent on 24 March 1988. Attempts to repeal Section 28 were implemented in election manifestos by the Labour Party in 1992 and the Liberal Democrat Party in 1997. Despite successive defeats to repeal Section 28 in the House of Lords, the Labour Government successfully passed the Local Government Act 2003 with the effect of abolishing this provision.

The impact of Section 28

No local authority was taken to court in breach of Section 28. The impact of the legislation nevertheless cannot be underestimated. Section 28 was never directly applicable to schools because it was targeted at local councils. Compounded by continual, erroneous reinforcement by sections of the media however, many working in education felt under the misapprehension that it did. They felt inhibited about what they could and could not say regarding sexuality. Most schools felt constrained in their abilities to challenge homophobic bullying. Consequently, Section 28 served to undermine the confidence of those professionals who sought, and had responsibilities, to provide appropriate advice and support to all young people and colleagues, especially lesbian, gay or bisexual people on the subject of same-sex relationships.

The legacy of Section 28

The repeal of Section 28 in 2003 was a watershed moment not only in terms of equalities legislation but also as a barrier to social change.

Since its repeal there has been more positive legislation and policy initiatives implemented particularly with regards to challenging homophobic bullying. The cast of Section 28's shadow did not end, however, with its repeal in 2003. Confusion continued to abound amongst many education professionals about what they could and could not say with regards to sexuality largely because the 2003 Labour Government specifically requested that political lobbying organisations refrain from trumpeting its repeal: fearful as it was at the time of a backlash from elements of the right-wing tabloid press. Indeed, in 2004 Bristol City Council was the only local authority in the United Kingdom to issue specific guidance to its schools on the implications of the repeal of the legislation and what it meant for their practice, commissioning EACH's Jonathan Charlesworth to write *Out of the Shadow* (Charlesworth, 2004).

The enduring influence of Section 28 on school practice was highlighted during the summer of 2013 when 44 schools across England were found to include statements prohibiting the 'promotion of homosexuality' in their sex and relationship education policies.

Signposting

Albert Kennedy Trust (AKT)

AKT supports LGBT 16–25-year-olds who are made homeless or are living in a hostile environment.
www.akt.org.uk

Anti-Bullying Alliance

A coalition of organisations and individuals working together to stop bullying and create safe environments in which children and young people can live, grow, play and learn.
www.anti-bullyingalliance.org.uk

Brook

Brook provides free and confidential sexual health services and advice for young people under 25.
www.brook.org.uk

Bullying Intervention Group (BIG)

BIG is a social enterprise established to administer the BIG Award and promote excellence in bullying intervention.
www.bullyinginterventiongroup.co.uk

ChildLine

ChildLine is a private and confidential counselling service for children and young people up to the age of 19.
www.childline.org.uk

Child Exploitation and Online Protection Centre (CEOP)

CEOP works with child protection partners across the UK and overseas to identify the main threats to children and coordinates activity against these threats to bring offenders to account.
www.ceop.police.uk

Educational Action Challenging Homophobia (EACH)

Since 2003, EACH have been the nation's dedicated provider of a dedicated actionline for young people to report and secure help further to homophobic or transphobic bullying. EACH is also a registered charity delivering training and consultancy to schools, colleges, universities, children and young people's services and other private, public and charitable sector organisations. EACH works with agencies to increase understanding of sexual orientation, gender identity and online safety whilst helping them respond to and challenge homophobic, transphobic or cyber harassment in a variety of settings.
www.each.education

Gender Identity Research and Education Society

This organisation provides information for transsexual people, their families and the professionals who care for them.
www.gires.org.uk

Gendered Intelligence

Gendered Intelligence is a community interest company that looks to engage people in debates about gender. They work predominantly within young people's settings and have educative aims.
http://genderedintelligence.co.uk

PSHE Association

This is the subject association for personal, social, health and economic (PSHE) education aiming to raise the status, quality and impact of PSHE education for all children and young people.
www.pshe-association.org.uk

Sex Education Forum

This is a group of organisations and individuals committed to improving sex and relationships education (SRE) for children and young people.
www.sexeducationforum.org.uk

References

Aiden, H., Marston, K. and Perry, T. (2013) *Homophobic Bullying: How Well Do We Understand the Problem?* Bristol: EACH.

Askew, S. and Ross, C. (1988) *Boys Don't Cry: Boys and Sexism in Education.* Maidenhead: Open University Press.

Benton, T. (2011) *Sticks and Stones May Break my Bones But Being Left on My Own is Worse: An Analysis of Reported Bullying at Schools Within NFER Attitude Surveys.* Slough: NFER.

Brook, PSHE Association and Sex Education Forum (2014). *Sex and Relationship Education (SRE) for the 21st Century.* London: PSHE Association.

Carr, A. (2014) *PinkNews.* London: PinkNews. Available at www.pinknews.co.uk/2014/04/16/alan-carr-the-most-homophobia-i-get-is-from-gays/ accessed on 29 October 2014.

Charlesworth, J. (2004) *Out of the Shadow: Guidance to Bristol Schools on the Repeal of Section 28.* Bristol: Bristol City Council.

Church of England Archbishops Council Education Division (2014) *Valuing All God's Children: Guidance for Church of England Schools on Challenging Homophobic Bullying.* London: Church of England Archbishops Council.

DCSF (Department for Children, Schools and Families) (2007) 'Homophobic bullying.' In *Safe to Learn: Embedding Anti-bullying Work in Schools.* London: DCSF. Available at www.each.education/wordpress/wp-content/uploads/2012/02/Safe-to-Learn-Homophobic-Bullying.pdf, last accessed 27 November 2014.

DfE (Department for Education) (2010) *FOI Release: Maintained Faith Schools* London: Department for Education. Available at www.gov.uk/government/publications/maintained-faith-schools/maintained-faith-schools, accessed on 11 June 2014.

DfE (Department for Education) (2012) *Exclusions from Maintained Schools, Academies and Pupil Referral Units in England.* London: Department for Education.

DfE (Department for Education) (2013) *Teachers' Standards: Guidance for School Leaders, School Staff and Governing Bodies.* London: Department for Education.

DfE (Department for Education) (2014a) *Mental Health and Behaviour in Schools: Departmental Advice for School Staff.* London: Department for Education.

DfE (Department for Education) (2014b) *Behaviour and Discipline in Schools: Advice for Headteachers and School Staff.* London: Department for Education.

US Department of Health and Human Services (2011) *Working With Young People Who Bully Others: Tips for Mental Health Professionals.* Washington: Department of Health and Human Services.

DeWitt, P. (2012) *Dignity for All: Safeguarding LGBT Students.* Thousand Oaks, CA: Corwin Publishing.

EACH (2014) *Reach Teaching Resource: A Practical Toolkit for Challenging Homophobic, Sexist and Cyberbullying.* Bristol: EACH.

East Sussex and Brighton & Hove PSHE Advisory Team (2002) The Sexuality Project: A Resource and Guidance Pack. Brighton and Hove: PSHE Advisory Team. Available on p.28 of www.gires.org.uk/assets/Schools/DCSF-01136-2009.pdf, accessed on 27 November 2014.

Glasser, W. (1975) *Reality therapy: A New Approach to Psychiatry.* New York: Harper Collins.

Goddard, A. and Patterson, L. (2000) *Language and Gender.* London: Routledge.

Hill, S. (2010) *The No-Nonsense Guide to Religion.* Oxford: New Internationalist Books.

Katz, A. (2013) *The Suffolk Cybersurvey.* London: Youthworks Consulting.

Kosciw, J.G., Greytak, E.A., Bartkiewicz, M.J., Boesen, M.J. and Palmer, N.A. (2012) *The 2011 National School Climate Survey: The Experiences of Lesbian, Gay, Bisexual and Transgender Youth in our Nation's Schools.* New York: GLSEN.

LGBT Youth Scotland (2006) *Toolkit for Teachers: Dealing with Homophobia and Homophobic Bullying in Scottish Schools.* Edinburgh: Learning Teaching Scotland.

London Borough of Wandsworth Safeguarding Children Board (2012) *Anti Bullying Strategy*. London: Corporate Communications Unit.

METRO Youth Chances (2014) *Youth Chances Summary of First Findings: The Experiences of LGBTQ Young People in England*. London: METRO.

Monk, D. (2011) 'Challenging homophobic bullying in schools: the politics of progress.' *International Journal of Law in Context* 7, 2, 181–207.

Nansel, T.R., Overpeck, M., Pilla, R.S., Ruan, W. J., Simons-Morton, B., Scheidt, P. (2001). 'Bullying behaviors among US youth: Prevalence and association with psychosocial adjustment.' *The Journal of the American Medical Association, 285*, 2094–2100.

NSPCC (2014) NSPCC Information Service (personal communication, 15 April).

Office of National Statistics (2011) *Religion in England and Wales*. London: Office of National Statistics.

Ofsted (2012) *No Place for Bullying: How Schools Create a Positive Culture and Prevent and Tackle Bullying*. Manchester: Ofsted.

Ofsted (2013) *Religious Education: Realizing the Potential*. Manchester: Ofsted.

Ofsted (2014a) *Exploring the School's Actions to Prevent Homophobic Bullying*. Manchester: Ofsted.

Ofsted (2014b) *Inspecting E-safety in School*. Manchester: Ofsted.

Olsen, W. and Welby, S. (2004) *Modelling Gender Pay Gaps: Working Paper Series. No. 17*. Manchester: Equal Opportunities Commission.

PETA (2014) *Be a little Fairy for Animals advertisement* [online advertisement], 15 April 2014. Available at http://blog.peta.org.uk/2014/04/alan-carr-be-a-little-fairy-for-animals, accessed 1 November 2014.

Renold, E. and Tetlow, S. (2013) *Boys and Girls Speak Out: A Qualitative Study of Children's Gender and Sexual Cultures*. Cardiff: Children's Commissioner for Wales.

Rogers, T. (2012) *The invention of the heterosexual*. San Francisco: Salon. Available at www.salon.com/2012/01/22/the_invention_of_the_heterosexual/, accessed on 31 October 2014.

Save the Children (2008) *Leave It Out: Developing Anti-homophobic Bullying Practice in School*. Belfast: Save the Children.

Tolman, D. (2009) *Dilemmas of Desire: Teenage Girls Talk about Sexuality*. MA: Harvard University Press.

Unilever (2014) *Advertisement for Cornetto ice cream* [online advertisement], 14 May 2014. Available at www.youtube.com/user/cornettouk

Webster, L (2009) 'Lottery grant to Bristol gay teens' group "outrageous"', *Bristol Evening Post*, 27 August 2009, p.1, www.bristolpost.co.uk/Lottery-grant-Bristol-gay-teens-group-outrageous/story-11246417-detail/story.html, accessed on 2 July 2014.

Weiler, E. (2003) *Making School Safe for Sexual Minority Students*. Bethesda: National Association of School Psychologists.

Wells, K. (2014) *NoHomophobes.com*. Available at www.nohomophobes.com, accessed on 29 November 2014.

Welsh Government (2011) *Respecting Others: Homophobic Bullying Guidance Document*. Cardiff: Welsh Government.

Woodward, A.J. (2014) *Dick Emery's Comic Characters: Confusing the Polarity* Available at www.woodysnet.co.uk/people/dick-emery/dick-emery, accessed on 2 July 2014.

Y Net News (2014) *Gay haredim lead double life, survey shows*. Tel Aviv: Y Net News. Available at www.ynetnews.com/articles/0,7340, L-4527108,00.html, accessed on 31 October 2014.

Index